# Stop Managing, Start Coaching!
## How Performance Coaching Can Enhance Commitment and Improve Productivity

Jerry W. Gilley, Ed.D.

Nathaniel W. Boughton, M.A.

**IRWIN**
*Professional Publishing*®
Chicago • London • Singapore

**Irwin Professional Book Team**

Publisher: *Wayne McGuirt*
Senior sponsoring editor: *Cynthia A. Zigmund*
Marketing manager: *Kelly Sheridan*
Managing editor: *Mary Conzachi*
Production supervisor: *Dina Treadaway/Carol Klein*
Manager, direct marketing: *Rebecca S. Gordon*
Compositor: *Electronic Publishing Services, Inc.*
Typeface: *11/14 Palantino*
Printer: *Quebecor Book Group*

**Times Mirror**
**Higher Education Group**

Library of Congress Cataloging-in-Publication Data

Gilley, Jerry W.
　　Stop managing, start coaching! : how performance coaching can
　enhance commitment and improve productivity / Jerry W. Gilley,
　Nathaniel W. Boughton.
　　　p.　　cm.
　　Includes index.
　　ISBN 0–7863–0456–1
　　1. Employees—Training of.　2. Employee motivation.　3. Mentoring
　in business.　4. Labor productivity.　5. Performance standards.
　I. Boughton, Nathaniel W.　II. Title
　HF5549.5.T7G476　1996
　658.3'124—dc20　　　　　　　　　　　　　　　　　　　　95–41399
　　　　　　　　　　　　　　　　　　　　　　　　　　　　　　CIP

*Printed in the United States of America*

2 3 4 5 6 7 8 9 0 Q 2 1 0 9 8 7 6

# *Preface*

The backbone of every organization, large or small, is its managers. They guide and direct employees' actions, decisions, and energies. They serve as friends and leaders, motivators and disciplinarians, confronters and counselors, and partners and directors. At the heart of their effort is the betterment of their employees and the organization.

In the history of war, every great army has relied on its field generals, the sergeants, to rally and direct the troops during battle in order to win the day. Every great basketball team has had *its* point guard to steer them to victory. Super Bowl champions have always had a quarterback who could work miracles on the field. All of these examples represent the value and importance of players who lead their teams in accomplishing greatness. In business, government, education, and industry these leaders are their managers.

Managers have direct contact with the people who do the work. They serve as liaisons between executives and employees. Managers interpret the organization's vision and communicate the messages given by executives. They are responsible for performance improvement, quality, and productivity. In short, managers are the ones responsible for getting things done and achieving the results needed by the organization. During the past decade, organizations have eliminated layer upon layer of managers in an attempt to become more efficient and productive. In the late 1980s, midlevel managers were an endangered species. Many organizations now realize that cutting the "managerial fat" has only allowed them to address the symptoms of their problem. Facing a new dilemma known as the "rightsized flat organization," organizations must finally address the real problem they face.

That real problem is the same old problem that has plagued organizations for years, one that has become the Achilles heel of thousands of organizations. It's not inadequate financial or strategic planning. It's not having too many managers. The real problem facing organizations is what we call "managerial malpractice." Simply stated, managerial malpractice is maintaining and using managers who are unqualified, poorly trained, misguided, or inadequately prepared—managers who do not have the interpersonal skills required to enhance employee commitment and improve organizational performance.

A new era has dawned for today's managers. Gone are the managers who spent their days planning, organizing, directing, and controlling. In their place is a new breed of manager who must use appropriate interpersonal skills to motivate and inspire their employees—and who must build relationships where the whole is greater than the sum of the parts. Managers must now develop healthy and positive working relationships to enhance the self-esteem and confidence of employees. Managers must be responsible for training employees so they can perform to the best of their abilities. Managers must provide career coaching in order to help employees enhance their careers, thus increasing their commitment to the organization. Managers must be responsible for confronting their employees in such a way as to improve their performance and quality. Managers must be responsible for mentoring employees so that they become the best they can be. Managers must understand the key to improving organization performance is to create work environments that enhance and develop the self-esteem of all employees. At the same time, they must create work environments that provide opportunities for their own personal growth and development. Managers must understand the importance of rewarding their employees for their contributions and performance.

In short we believe managers must *stop managing and start coaching* their employees in order to enhance commitment and improve productivity. We refer to this transformation as performance coaching. This book is dedicated to providing you, the reader, with a road map in becoming a successful and productive performance coach.

We begin our journey by discussing the failures of today's organizations. We examine four environmental conditions every organization faces, and how organizations respond to each. We discuss the need for a new organizational paradigm that helps your organization overcome managerial malpractice and replace it with professional managers.

In Chapter Two, we turn our attention to addressing managerial malpractice. We identify the attitudes, skills, and behaviors that contribute to this problem. We establish a solid case for changing the way you perform as a manager and provide the foundation for your transformation to performance coach.

The performance coaching process is overviewed in Chapter Three. We endeavor to discuss the entire process and provide you

### The Performance Coaching Process

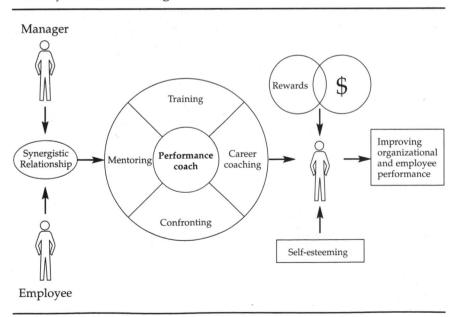

with a framework that will guide you during your journey in becoming a performance coach.

However, before you begin your trip, we pause to examine the principal barrier preventing the successful transformation from managing to performance coaching, which is today's human resources department (HRD) philosophy. This barrier helps us explain why employees are treated so poorly in so many organizations.

In Chapter Four, we explain the seven failures of today's HRD philosophy and provide solutions to each. We discuss the importance of reengineering the HRD function in order to enhance learning transfer so that performance can improve. We suggest that training be broken down into a modularized format to encourage and assure application. We provide strategies that will help your organization use its training professionals as internal consultants responsible for performance management systems.

The performance coaching process begins with the creation of a positive and healthy working relationship between you and your employees (Chapter Five). We identify nine components that are essential in creating this relationship. We explain how these components interact with one another and how they contribute to the formation of an "ownership attitude" on the part of employees. We discuss how you can use each of the nine components in forming better working relationships with your employees. The heart of the performance coaching process is the four roles in which you serve: training, career coaching, confronting, and mentoring. Each role has a number of different outcomes associated with it.

In Chapter Six, we begin by looking at the manager as a trainer. We discuss the importance of this role to improving organizational performance and efficiency. We explain why it makes so much sense to use managers as trainers and to shift the professional trainer's role to that of internal consultant. We discuss the need for managers to develop a training partnership with professional trainers in order to enhance employee and organizational performance. We identify the skills required to become an effective trainer. We also provide an overview of the training–learning process that includes the *seven laws of training*. We examine each law in detail and provide you with specific rules to follow to ensure success. We also discuss common mistakes and violations made by managers while executing each of the laws. Finally, we discuss several strategies that can be used in improving transfer of learning.

The role of career coach is overviewed in Chapter Seven. We outline the organizational benefits of career coaching, your career coaching advantages, and the career coaching process. The majority of this chapter is dedicated to the techniques and skills you must use to be effective in career coaching. One of the most important performance coaching roles to the organization is that of confronter (Chapter Eight). It is in this role that your entire attention is focused on improving performance and resolving problems. We identify three sets of skills essential in performing this role, and we explain how you can use these skills to improve employees' relationships as well as their performance. The three sets of skills are: assertion, conflict resolution, and collaborative problem solving.

The last role of performance coaching is that of mentoring (Chapter Nine). We believe that mentoring is one of the most important roles of the performance coaching process and that it requires the most skill. For mentoring to be successful, your relationship with your employees must be very positive. Your employees must respect your recommendations and suggestions. We provide you with 11 steps in successfully creating a mentoring relationship with your employees. Your success as a mentor depends on how well you develop each of these steps. We believe the primary outcome of the performance coaching process is a "self-esteeming" relationship between you and your employees. Self-esteeming is based on a collegial partnership between you and your employees where you feed off each other. Self-esteeming is also based on an enormously powerful need to feel good about yourself, your experiences, and your skills and abilities. In short, self-esteeming is the sum total of how you feel about yourself.

In Chapter Ten, we demonstrate how you can establish self-esteeming relationships with your employees. We discuss the many opportunities for self-esteeming and the four primary sources of self-esteem building. We teach you how to use these sources in enhancing and improving the self-worth of your employees. We also examine the impact of self-esteeming on teams and team development. Finally, we look at the organizational impact of self-esteeming relationships. We conclude our discussion of the performance coaching process by examining the reward strategies that help you get the results you need (Chapter Eleven). We begin by analyzing why employees behave the way they do. We outline three fundamental principles that explain most employee behavior. Next, we focus our attention on four reward strategies that enhance employee commitment and get results. We conclude our journey by discussing nine specific rewards that help improve performance and quality.

**Jerry W. Gilley**
**Nathaniel W. Boughton**

# Contents

## Chapter One

# The Failure of Today's Organization

Managerial fads have come and gone since the industrial revolution. Today managers are besieged with information about empowerment, total quality management, self-directed work teams, change management, reengineering, and the learning organization. These interventions attempt to cure all organizational ills. But in identifying the real causes of organizational failure, we see one simple theme that has handcuffed every organization. We call it *managerial malpractice.*

Managerial malpractice is simply encouraging and supporting practices that produce unprofessional, unproductive, and incompetent managers. Symptoms include (1) keeping managers who are not good at getting results through people; (2) promoting people to management who don't have the first clue how to manage; (3) selecting "new" managers because they are the best performer or producer without regard for their people skills; (4) spending valuable time fixing managerial incompetence instead of hiring qualified managers; (5) keeping managers who preach the importance of teamwork but then reward individuals who work at standing out from the crowd; and (6) allowing managers to say one thing and do another.

Organizations spend billions of dollars every year trying to solve managerial malpractice by applying every new fad that comes along. In the end, nothing ever really changes. The organizations still have performance problems and inefficiencies. They still lack the results required to be profitable.

Another growing disaster is the overreliance on personality instruments and profiles so that managers can get in touch with themselves and their people. While it's nice to read these "horoscope" descriptions of self, how do they really help managers relate to their employees, help them improve results, and help the organization achieve its goals and objectives? We don't believe they help the organization move in the right direction. What is needed is a dose of common sense, because the solution is right under our noses.

Managers must be selected for their people skills and must be held accountable for getting results through people. Managers must understand a simple rule of human nature: People produce more when they are given the tools and resources to get a job done, encouraged to provide input and suggestions, rewarded and recognized for their contributions, and treated with honor and respect. Simply, managers must build supportive and collaborative relationships with their employees.

In addition, the organization must get out of the way. It must let managers manage. It also must provide an environment that supports managers by continuously examining its operational focus and must make adjustments to ever-changing conditions in the internal and external environment. Finally, the organization must provide the training necessary to produce "professionalized" managers. We believe this is best done by teaching managers to become responsible for one-on-one and group interactions through performance coaching. After training, the managers who don't improve relationships with their employees or don't get the results required should not be allowed to remain as managers. Their employees deserve that much consideration.

In the next two sections of this chapter, we will overview several causes that contribute to organizational failure, and in the final section we will discuss the need to develop a new organizational paradigm.

## LACK OF ORGANIZATIONAL FOCUS

Can you imagine sailing a boat from one point to another without charting the course, without considering the wind direction or speed, without considering the ocean currents, and/or without considering future weather conditions? Failure to consider certain conditions could result in the loss of life. Changes in any of these conditions would also need to be communicated to your crew so they could take necessary action. If you wouldn't sail a boat without proper planning, it doesn't make sense to run a company that way.

Organizations that don't have a clear focus severely weaken their managers' ability to operate efficiently. Under these stressful conditions, many managers become even more demanding and forceful, which negatively impacts their relationships with their employees. In the end, the employees are unhappy, the managers are ineffective, and the organization can't get the results it needs. The organizational ship ends up crashed upon the rocks, never to sail again.

Mission, vision, and purpose are all terms used to describe organizational focus. Organizations endeavor to determine their focus in order to help them make critical decisions regarding their future. Once identified, the organizational focus serves as a reference point in helping managers direct their employees' energies.

All too often, the focus of organizations is unclear. To further complicate the situation, senior managers and executives fail to recognize that this is a problem. If left unchecked the problem could lead to disaster.

Another problem is that managers are often slow in communicating changes in focus to their employees. As a result, employees are forced to make decisions without clear information, which can lead to confusion, mistakes, and misunderstandings.

## ADJUSTING TO CHANGING CONDITIONS

One known and agreed-upon fact in today's organization is that change is going to occur. Change is a way of organizational life. The trick is to identify the type of change the organization is facing

**FIGURE 1.1**
*Overconfidence*

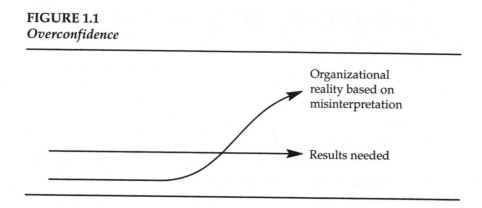

and to select the most appropriate response. We see four types of environmental conditions every organization faces at some point in its history. Each condition forces the organization to address a different law of economic disaster. The environmental conditions are (1) overconfidence, (2) crisis, (3) growth, and (4) equilibrium. In the remainder of this section, we will examine each condition and its corresponding law of economic disaster in more detail.

## Overconfidence

Many organizations face the environmental condition of overconfidence. It is one where the perceived reality greatly exceeds the results needed by the organization (see Figure 1.1). Overconfidence leads managers and executives to believe that they are invincible. In this type of environment, organizational leaders are not receptive to new ideas or ways of improving performance and quality. They believe the organization is untouchable, and without fault.

In an overconfident environment there is a tendency to rest and take it easy. The organization is not unlike a football or basketball team coasting in the second half because it has a big lead. The coaches often make a mistake by changing their game plan to protect the lead rather than executing the strategy that helped them build the lead. This change in the game plan may allow the

**FIGURE 1.2**
*Crisis*

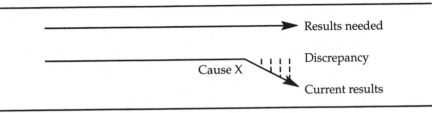

momentum to be captured by the other team. That is how upsets happen. We can all remember a team that lost a big lead, and the game, by playing too conservatively.

**Law of fast forgetting.**   In the wake of perceived success, managers tend to forget basic management principles. They forget how they became successful. They forget about their people and the contributions and sacrifices they have made. They lose sight of reality and fail to think about the future. They become short-term oriented instead of thinking about long-run profitability. They forget to invest in the training and development of their people, and they forget the importance of research and development to remain competitive.

An overconfident environment is caused by a false reading of the situation facing an organization. Managers must guard against overconfidence at all costs. They must continue to remind themselves of how the organization became successful and how to continue to apply sound management principles. Another way managers can protect against this condition is to keep accurate records and review them periodically. This helps prevent complacency.

### Crisis

Every organization eventually faces an economic condition where everything is going fine, the needed results are coming in, and all of a sudden the bottom falls out (see Figure 1.2). Something happened. Something went wrong. The first thing the organization does is to go into a period of shock. Managers don't know what to do. They're paralyzed, unable to move. After this wears off, they deny the situation ever really happened. They can't believe it is as bad as it really is. They don't search for the real causes of the problem because they are not convinced the situation is really real. Finally, if they're lucky, they wake up and begin to address the problem and its causes.

During a crisis, managers are looking for someone to blame. They are looking for a sacrificial lamb to offer up to senior management. This period is full of mistrust, poor communications, and finger-pointing. Teamwork and empowerment go right out the window. "Forget that stuff, it's my job I'm protecting" is the attitude of the day. Things are said that would be otherwise left unsaid. Fear and paranoia are the best words to describe the contents of the environment. No one is to be trusted.

A crisis produces stress for employees, managers, and executives—but not all stress is harmful. Stress can have a positive impact on productivity and performance. Figure 1.3 demonstrates the relationship between stress and productivity. As stress increases, productivity rises. Thus, stress is a positive stimulant for improving productivity. However, there is a point where stress goes too far and thereafter has a negative impact on productivity. We refer to this as an area of *distress*. Distress causes workers to perform less adequately; as a result, quality begins to slip. If distress continues, it produces a state known as burnout. Burnout is a condition that adversely affects individuals as well as productivity. Turnover is very likely and productivity greatly suffers.

**Law of slow learning.**    Sooner or later after a crisis, most organizations dig themselves out of their economic hole and begin to function normally. One thing they forget to do is heal the damage done by the crisis. We're not talking about the financial damage, but the emotional damage. Because employees don't trust managers, managers don't trust senior managers, and senior managers don't trust executives, an environment exists that requires

**FIGURE 1.3**
*Relationship between Stress and Productivity*

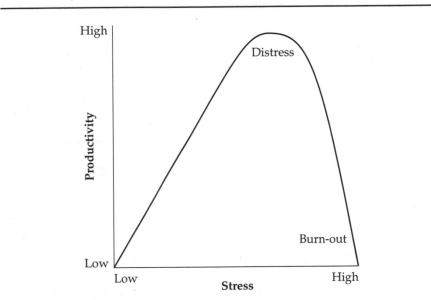

healing. Managers must make efforts to address the concerns of employees.

A period of crisis can provide an opportunity for managers to build strong long-term relationships with their employees. Through managers' efforts, a sense of bonding can take place. However, a period of crisis can be one of missed opportunities as well. Managers' failure to communicate and provide timely feedback to employees may cause irreversible interpersonal damage.

Often the biggest failure after a crisis is managers' lack of understanding that this type of condition will eventually happen again. Many are slow to learn from crisis conditions. Managers must guard against becoming paranoid but must learn from previous mistakes and must improve in the future. Otherwise they are doomed to repeat the same damaging behaviors as before.

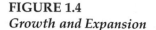

**FIGURE 1.4**
*Growth and Expansion*

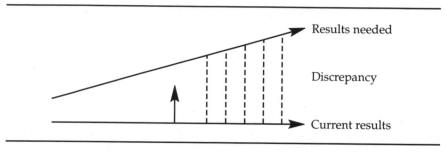

## *Growth and Expansion*

There's an old saying that describes the attitude of many managers: Grow or die. They are constantly striving for more. The quest for more is their primary motivator. It is a condition where today's results are not considered adequate to sustain future operations. There is a discrepancy between the results needed and today's reality (see Figure 1.4). All organizational efforts are focused on closing this gap.

During periods of growth, most managers are encouraged to hire as many people as needed to get the job done. So organizations stockpile employees like weapons during a war. The attitude is, the more the better, all shapes and sizes, all types—with little regard for matching performance skills with job requirements.

**Law of missed opportunities.**  During growth and expansion, however, there is no time to properly orient employees. Managers simply assist employees with the work to be done and tell them when it's due. The organization is too busy to provide adequate instruction. We have often heard managers tell employees, "You can figure it out, that's why we hired you."

Performance standards also are not used because managers are too busy managing and workers are too busy working. They don't have the time to identify the standards. Quality is another thing jeopardized during this period. Managers spend little time checking the final product. Their belief is that productivity will cure all other problems. This prevents them from understanding the future ramifications of their efforts.

During a period of growth and expansion, managers often miss many opportunities to develop their employees. They don't provide immediate feedback when employees don't perform properly. Conversely, they don't tell employees they've done a good job when they've exceeded expectations. By missing opportunities to communicate, managers fail to develop collaborative relationships with their employees.

One of the best examples of developing talent under pressure comes from Bobby Knight, basketball coach at Indiana University. Many people don't like his style, but he is the quintessential teacher. During the basketball championship in 1987, Steve Alford, Indiana's All-American point guard, tried to force the ball inside when there was an open man at the top of the key. The result was no points and the other team getting the ball. During the next play stoppage, Bobby Knight firmly explained to Alford what he had done wrong and how to correct it. He reminded Alford of his leadership responsibilities and challenged him to stay focused. Result: Alford hit three straight three-pointers and Indiana went on to win the national championship.

We describe this as a breakthrough moment—an opportunity for employees to learn immediately from a mistake. The learning is never forgotten and remains as a reference forever. The manager's primary responsibility in these situations is to maintain employees' self-esteem and confidence. *Distress* and *confusion* are words connected with periods of growth and expansion. Managers may miss opportunities to reduce employees' distress by not clearly communicating expectations. They should also provide feedback while employees perform their jobs. It helps employees know when they are performing their jobs correctly. Providing feedback is the least expensive and easiest method managers can use to improve employees' performance and to reduce their confusion.

During growth and expansion, managers sometimes fail to provide the adequate time to discuss the organization's intentions.

Employees feel shortchanged and left out of the loop. They begin talking among themselves, and this is how wild, unsubstantiated rumors begin within organizations. Employees deserve to know where the organization is going and how they fit into the organizational equation. It's their life that's being dealt with.

## Equilibrium

Occasionally, organizational life is like a calm lake in the early morning. The stillness is deafening. When this condition exists, the actual and needed results are in equilibrium (see Figure 1.5). The stress level in the organization is low, and production is only adequate. For many managers and employees, equilibrium represents a desired state of operations. However, new ideas and innovations are often resisted because managers and executives don't want to rock the boat. They're satisfied with the position of the organization and its future.

**Law of apathy.** While equilibrium is a desired state and may represent utopia, there are some serious consequences that can result. In Figure 1.3, we demonstrated the relationship between stress and productivity. Stress has a positive effect on productivity; conversely, the lack of stress can have a negative effect. It can produce a state of apathy, which can cause employees and managers to rest on their past accomplishments. In other words, the organization gets too comfortable and fails to maintain its competitive spirit. If this period lasts too long, disaster can result. The U.S. automobile industry offers proof of this phenomenon. Sears watched passively while Wal-Mart overtook it as America's number one retailer. The net result for Sears was the loss of thousands of jobs for long-time employees and midlevel managers—a very high price to pay for equilibrium.

The relationship between managers and employees has the potential of being at its best during equilibrium. However, the long-term effect could very well be unemployment. This is not a desired end. Therefore, managers must be responsible for innovations and

**FIGURE 1.5**
*Equilibrium*

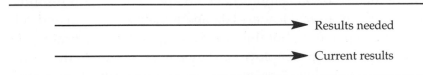

performance improvement during this period. They must recognize when apathy has taken root and must take corrective action to eliminate it. Maintaining an attitude of continuous improvement is one of the best ways of combating apathy. Liberating employees by transforming them from water into steam to run the engine through involvement and collaboration is essential. Apathy can be described as the enemy within, and all managers and employees must guard against it.

## DEVELOPING A NEW ORGANIZATIONAL PARADIGM

Too many organizations have failed in their pursuit of excellence. They have overextended themselves, and many companies today are "rightsizing" in order to survive. What happened? Who or what is to blame? What can organizations do to resolve the dysfunction of the past yet still remain competitive in the years to come?

The first step is to develop a new paradigm with real solutions to issues that affect all organizations. The new paradigm must help organizations overcome managerial malpractice and put into place a process designed to develop "professional managers." The results will be greater productivity, increased profitability, and improved organizational performance. Managers and employees will experience a better working relationship that will contribute greatly to the effectiveness of the organization.

### The Problem

Many of today's organizations have no apparent human resource strategy. Organizational leaders talk about their wonderful and colorful vision statements, but they are missing the most critical ingredient: buy-in from the employees. They pay lip service to the workers with comments like "Our people are our most valued resource." But most organizations use only 20 percent of the intellectual capital of their employees. We have seen repeatedly that when the best minds leave, an organization has great difficulty in sustaining itself.

The offensive left guard and the second seat trumpet player may not bring value in terms of hard dollars to a game or performance, but without them the team cannot perform up to its capabilities. The same concept must be employed within organizations. Each piece of the team is critical, and all are interdependent. Collectively and synergistically, success will be born.

Unfortunately, in many organizations not only is there no human resource strategy, but the current human resource development paradigm continues to fuel the failure of the organization. There has always been a dysfunctional relationship between human resource development professionals and management, because both groups tend not to understand their respective roles and responsibilities in the organization, that is, to manage and to develop the human factor. These professionals have failed miserably in "learning transfer," both because the wrong people are doing the training and because the training is not performance based. Finally, managerial malpractice is accepted by many organizations as standard operational procedure, which results in inefficiency, poor performance, dismal quality, and unproductive working relationships and work environments.

### The Solution

We need to create a new paradigm, one that will help create a winning organization by eliminating managerial malpractice. It will include the following:

1. Developing a new human resource development philosophy.
2. Modularizing training.
3. Creating transfer of learning strategies.
4. Using human resource development professionals as internal consultants responsible for performance management systems.
5. Enhancing employee relations and creating an ownership attitude.
6. Using managers as performance coaches to do training, career coaching, mentoring, and performance confronting.
7. Creating self-esteeming employees and teams.
8. Identifying reward strategies that motivate employees, improve their commitment, and get results.

These eight elements of the new paradigm are the components of the Performance Coaching Process, which will be the focus of the remaining chapters of this book.

## Chapter Two

# Eliminating Managerial Malpractice

We have all experienced the manager from hell: the manager who treats his or her employees like dirt. The manager who doesn't think you have had an original thought in your entire life. The manager who is indifferent toward his or her employees, has a superior attitude, and considers employees as something to use and abuse. The manager who has poor listening and feedback skills. The manager who couldn't develop a positive relationship with anyone. The manager who couldn't delegate, develop his or her people, conduct performance appraisals, or establish priorities. The manager who had a short fuse and little patience with you. The manager who criticizes you personally for the work you do. The manager who has created a work environment full of fear and paranoia.

If you have had a manager like this, you have experienced managerial malpractice. We don't need to tell you how destructive and damaging such a manager can be. The big question is how many of these attitudes, skills, and behaviors are you, as a manager, guilty of today? The answer rests between you and your employees.

Regardless, we would like to discuss managerial malpractice in more detail and provide some suggestions for addressing it. In Chapter 1, we identified six symptoms of managerial malpractice. We would now like to identify some of the attitudes, skills, and behaviors that contribute to managerial malpractice. Because we are moving our discussion from general to specific, we will be addressing you directly at different points throughout this chapter.

*Attitudes:*

1. Exhibiting indifference toward employees.
2. Feeling superior to employees.
3. Showing favoritism to certain employees.
4. Disregarding employees' worth.

*Skills:*

1. Poor listening skills.
2. Poor feedback skills.
3. Poor interpersonal relationship skills.

*Behaviors:*

1. Lack of performance appraisals and standards.
2. Ineffective delegation.
3. Lack of involvement in employee development.
4. Lack of patience with employees.
5. Criticism of employees rather than their performance.
6. Changing priorities and work requirements.
7. Creating a paranoid work environment.

Let's examine each of these contributing factors more closely.

## ATTITUDES

Your attitudes are made up of your beliefs and feelings toward something or someone. An attitude can't actually be observed because it is an internal mental state. However, attitudes serve as a guide to behavior. The behaviors associated with an attitude can be identified by anyone who observes interaction between people. Thus, attitudes are very important to you because they dictate the way you interact with and treat your employees.

## Indifference

Psychiatrists believe that the opposite of love is not hate but indifference. They contend that love and hate are very similar emotional states but with differing intentions. Indifference is an attitude of total disregard. In other words, a person who is indifferent toward another does not care what happens to that person and is not interested in his or her well-being. The indifferent person doesn't talk to the other person unless necessary, and the conversations are very formal, with little or no emotional involvement. The Spock character in "Star Trek" is a good example of a person with an indifferent attitude toward others. His lack of warmth and engagement is clearly observable.

Indifferent managers prohibit a positive relationship from being formed with their employees because they don't encourage communication. They don't want suggestions or recommendations given to them by employees. They prefer to be at arm's length when interacting with employees. Indifferent managers appear as if they would prefer not to work with people unless they have to. Employees resent indifferent managers because such managers make them feel insignificant. We heard a worker describe her feeling toward an indifferent manager this way: "He makes me feel small, like I don't exist. Talking to him is like pulling teeth—you can never get him to tell you what he thinks. If he wants to treat me this way, that's fine, who needs him . . . I'll just do my job, collect my paycheck, and go home." The danger of indifference in managers is that it produces indifference in employees. Indifferent managers negatively affect everyone who comes in contact with them.

## Superiority

A person with an attitude of superiority believes he or she is better qualified, more aware, or more insightful than most people. Superiority is a state of mind brought about through the experiences of life. People reflect on their experiences differently—some discount them while others inflate them. People with a superior attitude tend to view their own experiences as being of greater importance and value than those of other people. Over time, this produces an attitude that can be summed up by the statement "I'm better than you."

Many managers maintain an attitude of superiority toward their employees. "I'm better than you because I'm the manager" appears to be their attitude. Their own decisions and thoughts are the only ones they consider right. They use criticism and disapproving looks to demonstrate their superiority over employees. When assigning work, they communicate in an authoritative tone and tell employees what to do rather than asking for their input. Listening is difficult for these managers because they believe they are wasting their time considering the ideas of a less knowledgeable person.

Employees dislike managers with a superior attitude because such an attitude makes them feel inferior. They may even wonder who appointed that person to be God. Employees actually work to discredit and undermine the efforts of such managers just to create problems for them. Most employees don't confront this type of manager but use passive-aggressive behaviors to make managers' lives as miserable as possible.

### Favoritism

Favoritism is a positive bias toward a specific type of employee. The favored employee possesses specific characteristics and attributes preferred by managers. The favored employee may have a particular professional background or academic degree, may be of a specific ethnic group or a desired gender, may be expressive and flamboyant or serious and reserved. Regardless, favoritism is an unfair bias toward one group or person over another group or person.

It is difficult to eliminate favoritism. It is human nature to prefer certain behaviors, attributes, and characteristics over others. However, managers must be careful not to give preferred treatment to certain employees. Nonfavored workers will grow to resent and dislike those employees given special treatment. Beyond internal conflict between employees, favoritism will cause serious morale problems. Teamwork can never be achieved when favoritism is present.

## Disregarding Worth

Many managers disregard individual employees' worth and thus believe employees are easy to replace. They maintain practices and procedures that demonstrate this point of view. We recently observed two managers discussing a problem they were having with one of their employees. One of the managers said, "I have had several discussions with Mary about her attitude toward other employees. She just doesn't want to be a team player—she's selfish and self-centered." The other manager replied, "Fire her, put an ad in the paper, and find another assistant manager. It's not like she's irreplaceable—she has only been with the company six months. Cut your losses and find someone you can work with better."

Perhaps dismissing Mary is the best alternative. She may not be salvageable. But it's the overall attitude that concerns us. Human resources are costly to replace. Dismissal is disruptive to the organization, to managers, and to other employees. Dismissal is also damaging to the person being let go. It can be very traumatic.

Furthermore, an attitude that employees are easy to replace keeps managers from realizing their responsibility to develop and mentor their employees. It's what we call Pontius Pilate management, which is based on the belief that managers can just wash their hands of any consequences of their actions and decisions. It allows managers to fire people who don't exactly meet their expectations. Managers with this type of attitude might tell an employee, "There's lots of people looking for work, so if you don't like it here, hit the road." This attitude will kill employee morale and severely limit employee loyalty.

Managers must work with their employees to nurture and develop them. They must spend time getting to know employees and figuring out who has the potential to be successful and who truly does not. Managing people requires hard work.

## SKILLS

Managerial malpractice occurs when managers don't have the skills to build long-lasting and effective relationships with employees. Without these skills, managers will not be able to build the type of rapport needed to foster teamwork, encourage self-direction, and build trust. They will never be able to empower employees or to enhance employees' self-esteem without mastering these skills. Yet millions of managers don't possess a fraction of the skills needed to motivate and encourage their employees. Managerial malpractice continues because managers have poor listening, feedback, and interpersonal relationship skills.

### Poor Listening Skills

Poor listening is often listed as the number one cause of conflict between managers and employees. There are a lot of reasons for poor listening skills. Lack of concentration, physical barriers, visual distractions, hearing ability, personal bias, and communication style of the speakers are a few of the most common reasons for poor listening. With or without the proper skills, managers spend as much as 50 percent of their time listening. Good listening skills are therefore essential for managers to be effective.

The act of listening requires effort and concentration. Listening to employees intently can help managers more readily understand the content and intended meaning of employees' words. Moreover, since managers also demonstrate respect through effective listening, certain positive results can be predicted. Effective listening is the first step to building a positive and productive relationship with employees. We will provide a comprehensive review of ways to improve listening skills in Chapter Seven.

### Poor Feedback Skills

Feedback can come in a variety of forms. Feedback can be direct or indirect, verbal or written, solicited or unsolicited, and friendly or unfriendly. Whatever form it takes, it is important because it is essential to learning. It helps employees know when they are performing their jobs correctly. This information is the first step to improving quality, performance, and ultimately organizational effectiveness.

Giving feedback appears to be a very straightforward and simple skill; however, it's very difficult to master. Many managers take feedback for granted. They think employees know when they're performing their jobs correctly. Unfortunately, most do not. Most employees want feedback in order to reassure them that they're performing adequately.

We recently interviewed several employees of a large human resources consulting firm to determine why they hadn't been performing adequately. The number one reason cited was "I didn't know what I was supposed to do." Feedback is critical to overcoming such a problem.

There are four good reasons for giving feedback in an ongoing way:

1. It's a powerful way of motivating people.
2. Giving feedback helps managers build relationships with employees.
3. Giving feedback also provides documentation that helps managers identify employee strengths and weaknesses.
4. Timely feedback enhances business results.

After managers understand the reasons for giving feedback, they should consider how to give it in the best way. In order for positive feedback to work, the message should follow these guidelines:

- *Be specific.* Tell people exactly what they did that you liked.
- *Be sincere.* Superficial flattery won't work. People know when they are being conned.
- *Deliver feedback immediately.* Provide feedback on the spot as soon as you see the employee perform correctly.
- *Give individualized feedback.* Personalize your message to the employee. Make feedback special.

- *Give feedback frequently but randomly.* The more frequently an employee is reinforced for a desired performance, the stronger the performance will be. But once the desired behavior has been demonstrated, random reinforcement is more likely to strengthen it. Using an inconsistent reinforcement schedule will help the behavior become habitual.
- *Make feedback clear and concise.* Feedback must be understood by the employee receiving it. Therefore, the clearer and more easily understood it is, the more effective it will be.

### *Poor Interpersonal Relationship Skills*

Many conflicts between managers and employees arise because the managers have not established a positive relationship. We have heard managers say, "This is the way I am, take it or leave it, I'm not going to change." They have little understanding of the complexity of interpersonal relationships, nor do they care. That's managerial malpractice in action—in fact, that's the gold-medal level of managerial malpractice.

Allowing poor interpersonal relationships with employees may very well be the biggest sin of today's managers. The first premise that managers must understand is that their primary job is to get results through people. This requires working *with* people to obtain the results needed. Managers must build positive and productive working relationships with their employees. It is essential.

The process begins by establishing rapport with employees. Rapport means an open, honest relationship. It is not superficial but rather indicates a deep concern for the well-being of employees. It is established through sincere interest in and acceptance of employees. It can be observed when managers are as concerned for the relationship they have with their employees as they are for the results the employees produce.

Building employee relationships is such an important component to overcoming managerial malpractice that we will discuss it in greater detail in Chapter Five.

## BEHAVIORS

We believe that behavior is the outward expression of internal thoughts and beliefs. In other words, thoughts become actions. It's easy to tell people that things are important, but actions define what is truly important. Managerial malpractice is present when there is significant difference between what managers say is important and what they actually do. The following sections briefly discuss seven behavioral violations of managers.

### Lack of Performance Appraisals and Standards

Imagine you're an experienced pilot flying at night during a storm, but your instruments have failed. You're flying blind. Your radio is out so you can't call the tower and determine where you are, you can't ask the air traffic controllers to tell you your altitude, your direction, or the conditions of the runway. The only information you receive is an occasional radio message that says, "You're doing OK." Are you feeling a little anxious?

This is exactly how employees feel when managers don't give them feedback regarding their performance. They don't know where they are, how they're doing, or whether or not they are producing the right results. They certainly don't know if they're producing the results on time or at the correct level of quality unless they are told.

Performance appraisals are a powerful tool to help managers communicate with employees regarding their performance. They also help managers recognize employees' strengths and achievements during the past year, as well as identify areas for growth. The performance appraisal process helps managers define performance goals and action plans for the next year. Finally, they help managers compare their expectations with employee performance.

Performance standards are simply the criteria used to determine what level of performance is acceptable. They serve as a checklist for quality and performance. Let's return to our previous example: The airline industry maintains a comprehensive check-list that each airplane must pass prior to taking off. If the plane fails to meet all of the standards, it is not allowed to depart. The reasons are apparent. Performance standards help employees monitor their own performance. They also help employees determine when they need help or guidance. Performance standards serve as a fail-safe system for quality, and it's the manager's responsibility to identify and communicate them to employees.

## Ineffective Delegation

One of the manager's biggest fears is in delegating work to employees. When we have asked managers to explain why this is true, they tell us several interesting things. For example: "It takes twice as long to explain how to do it as it would take to do it myself," "They'll screw it up," and "I don't think they can do it as well as I can." All of these are miserable excuses. Remember, the manager's job is to produce results through people. Managers must delegate to be successful.

We define delegation as *appointing someone to operate on one's behalf.* This means the employee will serve as the manager's replacement and will perform the task for him or her. The employee functions as a pinch hitter in the late innings of a close baseball game.

Delegation involves three basic concepts: responsibility, authority, and accountability. Responsibility refers to the job assignment—the intended results. Authority refers to the right to act and make decisions that are necessary to achieve the intended result. Accountability means being called on to answer for actions and decisions made by the employee.

An effective manager must delegate an appropriate level of authority to accomplish a task and must clearly communicate what is to be done. Two things must be present before a manager can delegate a task. First, the employee must have the skills and ability to successfully complete the task. Second, the manager must have confidence in the employee's skills and abilities. In other words, delegation doesn't occur unless there is *trust* between managers employees. Lack of trust is the primary reason managers fail to delegate. Managers must develop trust in their employees before delegation can be successful.

To begin improving your own delegation skills consider the following guidelines:

1. *Decide what to delegate.* Who is qualified? What support or training do they need?

2. *Plan the delegation.* Review all essential details and decisions, determine appropriate feedback controls, provide for training and coaching, and establish performance standards.

3. *Select the right person.* Consider the employee's interests, skills, and abilities. Is the person qualified to complete the assignment?

4. *Delegate effectively.* Clarify the results you want and priorities involved, clarify the level of authority granted, clarify the importance of the assignment, and clarify feedback and reporting requirements.

5. *Follow up.* Insist on results, but not perfection; insist on timely performance and reports. Encourage independence— don't short-circuit or take back assignments. Reward good performance.

### *Lack of Involvement in Employee Development*

Most workers hired by organizations have entry-level knowledge and skills. While these are adequate to begin with, they are not sufficient to meet ever-demanding performance expectations and provide employees with future career opportunities. Managers who fail to help employees acquire the knowledge and skills needed to advance within an organization severely handicap their employees. They prevent them from developing their full potential and realizing true job satisfaction.

The organization also suffers when managers fail to develop employees. Organizations can't remain competitive unless their employees improve their performance and quality. By not developing employees, managers may be holding the organization hostage. The very future of an organization is linked to the development of its human resources.

We will examine the role of managers as trainers in Chapter Six. We will look there at the duties and responsibilities of managers in this role and will examine the importance of training professionals in tomorrow's organization. We will also look at the underlying principles that help managers as trainers understand how employees learn.

### Lack of Patience with Employees

Have you ever had a manager who assigned you a task to be done but couldn't leave you alone to complete it? Have you ever had a manager who explained a complex procedure to you and expected you to perform it perfectly the very first time? Have you ever had a manager who wouldn't let you completely explain an idea before interrupting you with a thousand questions? Have you ever had a manager who couldn't stand to see you complete a task without trying to do it for you? If you have experienced any of these behaviors, you know how difficult it is to work for an impatient manager. Such managers make you feel bad about yourself. They minimize your effectiveness and confidence.

Managers often expect employees to perform without needing guidance or direction. They believe employees should be able to do their jobs without conflict. Many managers don't want to be bothered with supervising their employees. However, most employees can't be expected to perform their jobs like clockwork or to interact with other employees without some tension. Employees are human. They make mistakes and errors. They require oversight and supervision.

Since employees don't come with instruction manuals or guarantees, it is your job to train and develop them. However, employees have a great deal of pride, which could be jeopardized when new tasks and jobs are assigned. They don't want to be embarrassed or ridiculed.

Employees need supportive and positive learning environments, and they will respond well to positive feedback. Employees also learn at different rates, and you must be patient with them during the learning phase. Remember, employees don't have the same level of experience and skills that you do. You must let them develop at their own pace.

### Criticism of Employees Rather Than Their Performance

Some managers delight in correcting their employees' performance. They enjoy letting them know when they've made a mistake or error. They may also personalize their criticism. Rather than focusing on the inappropriate performance, mistakes, or errors, they verbally attack employees. They think nothing of criticizing employees in front of their co-workers because they believe that a public repudiation has a positive influence on future performance.

However, maintaining the self-esteem of employees is absolutely critical when building strong employee relationships. When you criticize an employee you should not make it personal. Correcting an employee's performance is part of a manager's job, but there is no reason to make it personal. Two hundred years ago, John Woolman walked barefoot from Baltimore to Philadelphia. He did it to better understand the pain black slaves suffered when they were forced to walk barefoot over long distances. By putting himself in the slaves' place, he better understood what slavery meant to the slaves. He had empathy.

The word *empathy* comes to us as a translation of a word used by German psychologists, *Einfuhlung,* which literally means "feeling into." It is the ability to understand another person pretty much as he or she understands himself or herself. Empathic managers are able to crawl into another's skin and see the world through his or her eyes. They communicate in a nonjudgmental way. Becoming empathic is key to overcoming personal criticism of employees.

## *Changing Priorities and Work Requirements*

Some managers are constantly changing from one priority to another. They are just putting out one fire after another. We call such people *reactive managers.* They don't think about what is really important to them, their department, or the organization.

One main reason managers are not more successful at getting results is that often they simply do not have specific objectives. Many have dreams, hopes, or vague aspirations, but these are not objectives. Objectives are specific statements about desired results to which you are willing to commit yourself. Some managers don't think about objectives very much. They just respond. This is very confusing for employees and causes a great deal of their frustrations.

Determining objectives is not really very hard to do. You simply write down the results you want to achieve at some point in the future. These become the primary motives for your actions. Once you have clarified your objectives, consider your activities. Ideally, your activities should lead you to your objectives. If they don't, you're focusing on the wrong things. You may be busy, but you're not getting results. We call this an activity trap. Remember, it isn't your activities that are important, it's your results. Activities become important only when they relate to your objectives and help you produce good results.

Basically, setting priorities is easy. You decide on your objectives, then you determine what activities must be done to reach each objective. Those activities are your top priorities. If your priorities seem to be constantly changing it may indicate that you have (1) failed to accurately identify priorities in the first place; (2) based priorities on something other than importance; (3) tried to set priorities without first clarifying objectives; (4) lacked coordination between different jobs, or (5) been totally disorganized.

## *Creating a Paranoid Work Environment*

Work environments that are full of fear and distrust are very unpleasant, to say the least. They are not conducive to creativity or innovation. They are full of tension and anxiety. The primary by-product of this type of work environment is distress. It is impossible for employees to do their best work when they fear the manager. It's like working for the troll under the bridge.

However, some managers don't think they have done a good job managing until all of their employees fear them. This is simply wrong—another classic example of managerial malpractice. It just makes no sense to demonstrate this behavior.

In order to develop a positive environment conducive to sharing and support, managers must become more participatory. The participatory approach requires a gentle shift away from authoritarian control. It is one of the most difficult things for a manager to master because it requires the manager to have the courage to relinquish control and dominance over his or her employees. In this way management becomes less threatening to employees. Participation also allows employees to become involved, which helps them support their own decisions.

The participatory approach requires managers to understand the importance of having a positive working relationship with employees, and to realize that employees bring a great deal of experience to a situation, which is an invaluable asset to be acknowledged, tapped, and used. However, managers sometimes fail to understand that this asset can provide a wealth of information that would be beneficial in a working relationship. Such recognition is indeed difficult but is essential in the development of positive rapport.

The first step in developing a participatory approach is to create an environment where a free exchange of ideas and feelings is encouraged. The benefit of this type of environment is that employees feel secure. Employees will also realize that the lines of two-way communication are open.

## INGREDIENTS FOR SUCCESS

A closer examination reveals that certain key elements are needed for the proper sharing relationship to develop. These ingredients are essential to success. They include understanding, acceptance, and involvement.

What we mean by *understanding* is recognizing and correctly interpreting the feeling, thinking, and behavior of employees. While we realize that managers can't always fully understand their employees, we can say that understanding employees is essentially a process of sharing.

Acceptance is the basic attitude managers must hold toward employees. It requires respect for employees as persons of worth. Managers can demonstrate acceptance by being willing to allow employees to differ from one another. This willingness is based on the belief that each employee is a complex person made up of different experiences, values, and attitudes.

A manager's willingness to care and feel responsible for employees is rightly called involvement. While acceptance and understanding are passive, involvement implies action; it means active participation in the employee's problems and needs. Only active and involved managers can become agents of change. This requires face-to-face contact with employees. Performance coaching, the subject of Chapter Four, will provide you with this necessary contact.

Managerial malpractice can be resolved through the Performance Coaching Process, which is a process designed to improve organizational and employee performance. The outcome will enhance the relationship between managers and their employees.

*Chapter Three*

# The Four Phases of Performance Coaching

*The Performance Coaching Process*

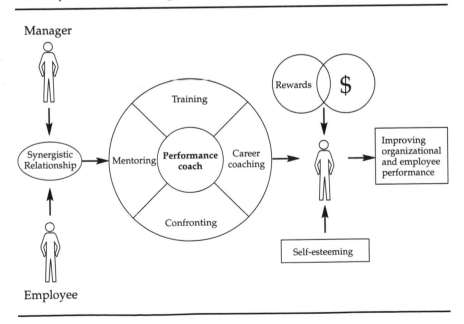

Performance coaching is "person-centered" management. It requires you to become involved with your employees by establishing rapport and encouraging face-to-face communications. Performance coaching is an active process requiring you to constantly shift from one role to another. It forces you to be an active participant with your employees rather than a passive observer. Performance coaching relies more on good questioning, listening, and facilitating skills than on assigning work and controlling outcomes.

Performance coaching is also a series of one-on-one exchanges between you and your employees. The purpose of each exchange is to help you solve problems, improve performance, or get results. These are straightforward responsibilities of every manager and have been a part of their duties since the evolution of management.

• *Solving problems.* Classic problem solving begins with identifying the conditions and factors that contribute to the problem. This is followed by identifying the solutions to problems and analyzing them. The solution that will best resolve the problem is then selected and implemented. Finally, the solution is evaluated to determine whether the problem was in fact solved. We believe that this process is a sound one with a proven track record. But we believe that employees must be integrated into the problem-solving process. They must be used as resources in problem solving and must be taught the skills required to apply problem-solving techniques on the job.

• *Improving performance.* Improving performance is a three-stage process. It begins by identifying performance standards and communicating them to employees. These standards serve as criteria to be used to determine whether or not a job is being conducted correctly. They also serve as a guide in executing the job or task.

The second stage is measuring current performance against the established performance standards. The purpose is to determine whether there is a difference between actual performance and desired performance. Regardless of the outcome, a record should be kept for future reference.

After performance evaluation comes the third stage of improving performance. If deficiencies exist, changes must be made in the way a job is being performed. Changes might include new procedures or processes. In some cases, actual performance will exceed the performance standards. Changes should still be made to ensure that high levels of productivity continue. If there is no significant difference between actual performance and desired performance, appropriate adjustments are still needed to ensure continuous improvement.

The three-stage process of improving performance also applies to people. Employees who fail to meet performance standards may need additional training to improve their competencies for a particular job. It may be determined that they will never be able to perform to standards and therefore need to be reassigned to another job. Employees who exceed performance standards need to be studied in order to determine what skills, abilities, or characteristics they possess that enable them to perform at such a high level. This information can be used in future recruiting and selection activities as well as in future training activities for employees.

Together you and your employees can participate in the process of improving performance. Employees should be used to help determine performance standards, measure actual against desired performance, and identify changes in performance processes and procedures. Only then will you obtain their buy-in into performance improvement. You should get used to facilitating each of the three phases because you will ultimately be held accountable for the performance of your employees.

- *Getting results.* Organizational leaders usually don't care how results are obtained. They just want the results they need. It is then your responsibility, as a manager, to get results. Results could include increasing sales, obtaining more units of production, increasing client service, or increasing market share—regardless, you must obtain results. You cannot obtain these results by yourself. You must rely on your employees. This is where the management dilemma begins. You must get results through people.

As we shared in Chapter Two, managerial malpractice is common in most organizations. We believe that in order to get the results they need, most managers must change the way they now manage. They must become performance coaches.

## PERFORMANCE COACHING IN ACTION

The performance coaching process consists of four interdependent phases. Each phase serves as the foundation for the next step. It is almost impossible to move forward unless the previous phase has been completed. The final phase serves as a reinforcer to the entire performance coaching process.

The four phases are as follows:

1. Developing a synergistic relationship with employees.
2. Using the four roles of performance coaching.
3. Developing self-directed and self-esteeming employees.
4. Selecting rewards that build commitment and get results.

In the following section, we will discuss the four phases of performance coaching in detail, and we will be addressing you, as the manager, directly throughout the discussion.

### *Developing a Synergistic Relationship*

The performance coaching process begins with the creation of a positive working relationship between you and your employees, one that enhances employees' commitment to improving performance and quality, increasing productivity, and organizational performance. Such a relationship produces a synergistic relationship with employees (see Chapter Five).

Let's look at this definition in its separate parts. A positive working relationship is one that benefits all parties. All members receive the specific outcomes they desire. But remember that it is a professional relationship, not a personal one. We are not suggesting that you become your employees' best buddy and pal but that you maintain a professional approach toward working together with them. What we mean by "enhancing their commitment" is for employees to be willing to make personal sacrifices to reach their team's, department's, or organization's goals. In order to accomplish this, you must clarify the goals of the team, department, or organization; provide the training necessary to obtain the competencies needed (see Chapter Six); and allow greater employee influence in decisions to be made regarding their jobs and careers (see Chapter Seven). In return for their enhanced commitment, you should reward employees appropriately (see Chapter Eleven). By creating work environments dedicated to continuous improvement through the self-esteeming of employees, (see Chapter Ten), you can improve performance and quality, increase productivity and organizational performance. We believe that employees who have an ownership share in the outcome of their organization will perform like an owner. It is your responsibility to produce this type of ownership attitude (see Chapters Eight and Nine).

## Using the Four Phases of Performance Coaching

During an exchange with employees, you will serve in one of four different roles: training, career coaching, confronting, and mentoring. Each role has a number of different outcomes associated with it. Let's briefly examine each of these roles and identify some common outcomes.

**Phase 1: Training.** In performance coaching, several roles are critical; however, none more so than the role of trainer. In this role, you will serve as a one-to-one teacher. You are responsible for sharing information that will ultimately impact the growth and development of your employees.

Some people would argue that you should not be responsible for full-time training because it's too time-consuming and intensive. They don't believe that you, as a manager, have the background to provide such things as interpersonal and communications skills

training, project and time management, or team-building and presentation skills. They believe that full-time trainers should be the
ones conducting training and you should merely supplement their
efforts.

We don't see it that way. You must get results through people
and therefore are the one responsible for the development of your
employees. Training should not be handed off to an outsider (i.e.,
professional trainer) who is not accountable for your employees'
performance. We believe performance and quality would improve
tenfold if managers were the ones training their employees.

We believe that you are the one most qualified to provide the
technical training needed by employees. In doing so, you can develop a greater awareness of the current skill level of your employees, including their strengths and weaknesses. Armed with this
information, you could develop priorities and plans for future development. We also believe that your interpersonal and communication skills would greatly improve as you train your employees.

Other skills such as listening and feedback could also be enhanced through the training role. As a trainer, you should communicate performance standards to your employees and should see
firsthand whether or not employees meet the performance standards. Any performance and/or skill gaps that are uncovered can
be addressed immediately. This would save time and improve
quality. If performance standards don't exist, it will be impossible
for you to determine the performance level of your employees.
When performance standards are absent, you and your employees
could identify them together. This will improve employee buy-in
and give you an opportunity to develop a better relationship with
your employees. Once performance standards are in place, you
and your employees will discover their importance as a measurement tool.

In Chapter Four, we will discuss the need for a new training
philosophy and delivery system in order for managers to become
trainers. We will also examine the role of the training professional
and the importance of learning transfer. We will also identify several strategies you can use to improve learning transfer.

Several outcomes can result through the training role:

- Increasing technical competence.
- Improving interpersonal interaction between managers and employees, and among employees.
- Improving problem-solving skills.
- Improving employee performance and quality.
- Enhancing relationships with employees.
- Increasing breadth of technical understanding.
- Improving competence of managers in technical and interpersonal areas through repetitive instruction.
- Developing commitment to continuous improvement and learning.

**Phase 2: Career coaching.** As a career coach, you will need help to guide employees through a reasonably in-depth review and exploration of their interests, abilities, and beliefs regarding their present and future career path. You will help employees consider alternatives and make decisions regarding their careers. You will also make the organization aware of your employees' career perspectives so that the organization can plan accordingly.

As with the trainer role, some people don't believe that you, as a manager, should be a career coach. They don't believe you are qualified to perform successfully and that you have some distinct disadvantages serving in this role. The disadvantages include employees' rights to privacy, and legal and ethical ramifications. We will discuss each of these in greater detail in Chapter Seven.

We believe you are in an excellent position to be a successful career coach. You have made career decisions similar to those facing your employees. Your experience can provide employees insight into the possible outcomes of their career decisions. You have real-life, practical experience on which to base your career recommendations, as well as a realistic appraisal of opportunities within the organization. You have established networks that can provide employees greater access to the information used in making career decisions. Finally, you have access to performance evaluation information on all your employees, which can be used in making realistic suggestions concerning career planning. This information can help you identify training activities that will help your employees overcome knowledge and skill deficiencies. Once skill deficiencies have been eliminated, organizational performance will improve. We will examine each of these advantages later in Chapter Seven.

We can identify several major outcomes of the career coaching role:

- Helping organizations identify performance deficiencies.
- Improving employees' insight regarding their career.
- Improving employees' insight about the organization.
- Helping employees make a greater commitment to their career and to the organization.
- Helping employees change their point of view about their career path.
- Helping employees to become self-sufficient and independent.

**Phase 3: Confronting.** The performance coaching role that is intended to improve performance is that of the confronter. There are two types of performance efforts you must make. First, employees must make positive adjustments in their performance. In other words, you want employees to improve on success. For example, you may want an employee to improve from a satisfactory level to an excellent level or to complete more complex and difficult tasks, such as increasing sales volume 15 percent or exceeding the performance standards for a particular job. However, be aware that employees often view this type of performance improvement negatively because it requires to them to work harder without increased financial rewards.

The second type of performance effort is more difficult. It requires you to move employees from an unsatisfactory to satisfactory level of performance. It is often embraced by employees because they appreciate the feedback; however, communicating unsatisfactory performance behaviors to employees is quite difficult. Telling your employees that they are not performing at a satisfactory level is perceived as a reprimand. Therefore, you must learn how to communicate performance improvement messages without criticism.

Confrontation is not criticism, but for confrontations to remain positive, you must (1) learn how to communicate specifically what you want employees to improve, (2) focus on the performance problem rather than on the person, (3) use confrontation to produce the desired change without causing the employee to become defensive, and (4) maintain a positive relationship with your employees. We will examine each of these in more detail in Chapter Eight.

The primary outcomes of the confronter role are to improve performance and communicate performance expectations. Other outcomes include:

- Identifying performance shortfalls.
- Identifying strategies for performance improvement.
- Obtaining commitment to continual improvement.
- Communicating performance standards.
- Performing more difficult tasks on the part of employees.
- Enhancing employee growth.

**Phase 4: Mentoring.** The mentoring role is the only role that can be initiated by you and/or an employee. It requires you to build a mutually trusting relationship with your employees. The mentoring role is the most difficult of the four performance coaching roles. For example, maintaining the integrity of the relationship between you and your employees requires the greatest people skills. Finally, mentoring is the only role that may be performed by other managers. In other words, you may serve as a mentor to your own employees or to those of another manager.

The primary purpose of mentoring is to help further the success of an employee's career. As mentor, you serve as a guide in helping the employee unlock the mysteries of the organization. You direct your employee through the perils and pitfalls of organizational life and help develop his or her political savvy.

The mentoring role differs from the career coaching role. Mentors act as a source of information on the mission and goals of the organization. Mentors provide insight into the organization's philosophy. Mentors teach employees how to function within the organization. Mentors serve as a confidant in times of personal crisis and problems. Career coaches don't focus on these activities but rather on how the employee's career is affected by the organization.

The mentoring role is also difficult because it requires you to share personal experiences with your employees in order to deepen their learning and understanding. Self-disclosures of this type are used to encourage employees. They demonstrate that you have had similar experiences and can relate accordingly. Also, they serve to remind employees that you have made mistakes that were learning opportunities and not career-ending events.

As a mentor, you should encourage your employees toward the appropriate risk-taking actions necessary for professional growth and development. This includes making statements that clearly encourage them to take actions to attain specific goals. It may even include encouraging an employee to transfer to another department or division within the organization.

Specific outcomes can be realized through the mentoring role:

- Developing employees' political awareness and savvy.
- Understanding and appreciating the specific nature of the organization's culture.
- Creating a personal network in the organization.
- Enhancing the relationship between you and your employees.
- Developing commitment to the organization's goals and values.
- Advancing the career of one or more employees.
- Increasing your involvement in the development of employees' careers.

## *Developing Self-Esteeming Employees and Teams*

The performance coaching process has as its foundation a collegial relationship between you and your employees. Such a relationship would ultimately enhance the self-esteem of your employees. A collegial partnership is a prerequisite in establishing and performing the four performance coaching roles.

*Self-esteeming* is the special word we use for the outcome of the performance coaching process. It comes from building up your employees' self-concept as a means of improving both their performance and their problem-solving skills. Self-esteeming is a process that benefits you as much as your employees because it encourages the development of a synergistic relationship between you and your employees.

The opportunities for self-esteeming occur daily in the world of your employees. You can draw from four sources in order to improve your employees' overall self-concept: (1) achievement, accomplishment, and mastery; (2) power, control, and influence; (3) being cared about and valued; and (4) acting on values and beliefs.

Improved performance and quality are common when the self-esteem of employees, not to mention that of the organization, is high. When self-esteem is low, the reverse is true.

Every team experience is a developmental process. The process corresponds with common emotions that every team must go through before it performs effectively. The phase/emotion process can be outlined as follows:

| *Phase* | *Emotion* |
| --- | --- |
| Forming | Anticipation |
| Storming | Anger |
| Norming | Acceptance |
| Performing | Renewed self-confidence |

We will examine these in more detail in Chapter Ten and discuss how each phase of team development affects the self-esteeming process.

Change is a constant in today's organization. As a performance coach, your role is to anticipate the changes that will impact your team. You must position yourself strategically within the organization to serve as a lighthouse of impending danger. You must be able, at a moment's notice, to adjust your game plan to account for these changes. The survival of your team depends on it. Organizations are like people; they are living systems. Organizations can experience high and low self-esteem. The self-esteeming process is as applicable for your organization as it is for your employees. The same four sources of self-esteem can be used to provide opportunities to enhance the organization self-esteem. The outcomes are almost identical. Organizations with high self-esteem demonstrate two-way communications, openness, trust, and a high commitment to human resources. Organizations with low self-esteem have low creativity, intragroup conflict, and win–lose attitudes.

### Selecting Rewards that Build Commitment and Get Results

Performance coaches and organizations must install compensation and reward systems that build commitment and improve the motivation of their employees. To accomplish this, we believe you must (1) understand the three basic principles of performance improvement, (2) develop an appropriate reward strategy, and (3) identify the types of rewards that achieve the best results.

We believe there are three basic principles of performance improvement:

1. The things that get rewarded are the things that get done.
2. It isn't what you expect that gets done; it's what you inspect that gets results.
3. If you're not getting the results you want, look at what's being rewarded.

The next step is to create a reward strategy that helps you get the results you want. In other words, organizations must be rewarding the right things. You must know what to reward and what not to reward. We believe that there are several behaviors performance coaches should be rewarding: risk taking, quality work, teamwork, independent decision making, applied creativity, loyalty, long-term solutions, and priority work.

As a performance coach, you should understand that not all rewards produce the same results. Therefore, it is important for you to know which rewards are the most effective. Some of the most effective are recognition, time off, favorite work, advancement, freedom and independence, and personal growth opportunities. One of the most controversial is financial rewards. We believe that money does make a difference but that you must understand the different types of compensation strategies that are available and the advantages of each. We will examine the following ones:

1. Gainsharing.
2. Small-group incentives.
3. Individual incentives.
4. Lump-sum payment/bonus.
5. Pay-for-knowledge.
6. Profit sharing.

In Chapter 11, we will examine the basic principles of performance improvement, the reward strategies, and the types of rewards that get results. We will also discuss the importance of each of these in building employee commitment and improving employee motivation.

## STANDARDS OF EXCELLENCE IN PERFORMANCE COACHING

In our experience the finest performance coaches create an environment that brings out the best in their employees. You can use the following criteria to create such an environment of excellence.

**Establish clear performance goals.** Performance coaches should help their employees establish clear performance goals. Performance goals will serve as a target to shoot for during the year. Encourage your employees to write out their goals and re-view them regularly. If you are coaching a team, help them create a mission statement for the project or group.

**Provide accurate feedback.**   One of your most important activities as a performance coach is to provide accurate informa-tion about your employees' performance. Improvements cannot be made unless your employees understand how well they are doing. Pat Riley, coach of the New York Knicks and formerly of the world champion Los Angeles Lakers, once said, "The job of a leader is to help people see reality."[1]

Give encouragement. Employees need to be reassured and sup-ported to maintain a positive outlook regarding their performance and contributions. Your job is to create an environment conducive to inspiration. You must give your employees the courage to change. In fact, the heart of the word en*courage*ment is courage.

**Be patient.**   One of the most difficult standards to meet is patience. It is very difficult to hold your tongue when employees don't perform to your expectations. You must remember that every person learns at a different rate. You must expect setbacks and plateaus as employees struggle to improve.

**Create a fear-free environment.**   In order to improve their performance, employees must learn new skills. They risk making mistakes and failing until they master the new skills. You must cre-ate a learning environment that is free of judgment and manipula-tion. Failure can be an excellent teacher. Encourage it.

**Expect success.**   Employee performance is dramatically affected by your expectations. You should expect employees ulti-mately to succeed. Yes, failure is possible as they acquire new skills, but employees sense your expectations of them. You must

---

[1]M.J. Gelb and T. Buzan, *Lessons from the Art of Juggling: How to Achieve Your Full Poten-tial in Business, Learning and Life* (New York: Harmony Books, 1994), p. 123.

believe in them as people and demonstrate your belief in the things you say, the tone of your voice, and the looks you give.

**Encourage excellence.** Challenge employees to perform at their personal best. By doing this you help them move beyond self-imposed boundaries to new levels of excellence. Challenging your employees to excel demonstrates your confidence in their ability to succeed.

**Ask questions.** Learning by doing is the most successful way for employees to learn. By asking your employees questions rather than telling them the answers, you force them to think. Questions promote a process of self-discovery and cause your employees to discover for themselves the correct answers. This approach will deepen your employees' commitment to what they have learned.

**Reduce ego involvement.** As employees work to improve their performance, you must guard against linking your own self-esteem to their performance. Their success or failure is not your own. You will remain accountable for their overall performance, but on balance you are not your employees and you must not define yourself by their actions.

*Chapter Four*

# Reengineering the Human Resource Development Process

As you examine the failure of corporations, countries, and empires, they all appear to have one thing in common. All of these institutions that failed did so because they did not adequately prepare for the future. Sadly, history repeats itself over and over again.

So why have the great leaders of industry and the world failed to plan for impending disaster? Let's consider the actions of a farmer to illustrate our point. When a farmer decides to plant a crop, what does he do? Does he take his seeds, throw them indiscriminately on the top of the soil, go back home, and wait for his bumper crop to come in? Or does he first prepare the soil for planting, plant the seeds deep into the earth, fertilize the soil soon after planting, irrigate the seeds if Mother Nature doesn't cooperate, weed the growing crop to ensure maximum growth, continue to fertilize and water the crop during the long hot summer months, and finally harvest the crop and prepare the soil for winter? The answer is obvious. Farmers work hard at producing their crop. They understand the relationship between strategic planning and the production of maximum yields.

Organizations must adopt the strategic planning approach of the second farmer in preparing for their future. However, the seeds of their effort are not better products and more capital, but their human resources. People are the organizational asset least developed and cared for—but they are the heart of every organization. Without their people, organizations would not be able to operate. They would not be able to service their customers. They would not be able to produce products or provide services.

Organizations are people, so why are people treated so poorly so much of the time? The answer is simple. Many organizations have the human resource development (HRD) philosophy similar to that of the first farmer. They think developing their human resources requires no effort. Their philosophy goes something like this: "We'll throw some training at our employees and hope that performance improves"; or "We really don't have the time to train and develop our people because we're so busy"; or "We'll get around to it as soon as we can; remember, the customer comes first"; or "If they don't develop fast enough or produce well enough we can find someone else who will." What organizations need is a new HRD philosophy, one that helps them prepare for the future in order to remain productive and competitive, one that improves organizational performance.

## THE SEVEN FAILURES OF TODAY'S HRD PHILOSOPHY

We believe that there are seven failures of today's HRD philosophy. Each of these contributes to the failure of organizations. They are as follows:

1. Failure to tie training to the organization's business objectives.
2. Failure to improve organizational results through training activities.
3. Failure to use an appropriate training approach.
4. Failure to use managers as trainers and agents of change.
5. Failure to use HRD professionals as internal consultants responsible for performance management systems.
6. Failure to train the right people for the right reasons.
7. Failure to transfer learning to the job.

## Failure 1: Not Connecting Training to the Organization's Business Objectives

Many HRD programs are not tied to the business objectives of the organization. When this occurs, training is being conducted in a vacuum. There is little focus on the problems facing the organization and how training can be used to address them. As a result, employees fail to receive the type of training they need to perform adequately. Organizational performance cannot improve because training is not focused on the business needs of the organization. We call this type of training the hit-or-miss approach. Some training is on target, but most isn't.

## Failure 2: The Activity versus Results War

HRD professionals can choose between two training strategies: (1) the activity strategy or, (2) the results strategy. These strategies differ in their focus and in their measurement of contribution to the organization.

Many HRD programs are designed to provide employees with a comprehensive and complete list of training courses. Little attention is paid to why employees participate in training as long as they attend some training class each year. Training is sometimes viewed as a reward for a job well done. We refer to this as the activity strategy of HRD.

HRD professionals who embrace the activity approach report the number of courses offered and the number of employees attending them as a way of measuring and validating their value. They believe that the more training that occurs, the better the organization will perform.

A results strategy is an approach HRD professionals use to improve organization performance through training. The focus is not on how many training programs can be delivered each year or on how many employees participated in training but on the results obtained through learning and skill transfer. HRD professionals who use this approach report on outcomes as a means of validating their programs.

The activity versus results war reflects the age-old argument of quantity versus quality, or the shotgun versus the rifle. We believe that training programs offered to employees as fringe benefits have little or no impact on organizational performance. HRD professionals who embrace the activity strategy believe improving organizational performance can occur if you throw out enough seeds (training programs). The activity strategy has a negative effect on the field of HRD and its professionals because organizational performance doesn't improve when this strategy is used.

### Failure 3: Inappropriate Training Approach

Traditional training is also a major problem for today's organization. Training usually involves taking a group of employees out of the work setting for a couple of days to a couple of weeks. This artificial environment usually doesn't resemble the workplace, creates an unnecessary barrier to the application of learning, and makes it much more difficult for employees to reproduce the skills learned. In addition, employees don't see the connection between training and their performance because training is often impractical and irrelevant.

Most training occurs in short time frames such as one or two days. So much information can be presented during this time that employees experience mental overload. According to research, as little as 20 percent of the information presented during training can be recalled by employees one month later. The amount of information recalled is a disappointing 2 or 3 percent three months after training. Why? One reason is that too much information is presented in too short a period of time. The average employee can't absorb it. To further complicate things, employees are expected to apply all they have learned to their respective jobs. The average employee gets confused and loses confidence. As a result, he or she doesn't transfer any of the information to the job.

## *Failure 4: Not Using Managers as Trainers*

In traditional training, the trainer is a professional who has subject matter expertise. He or she is employed by the organization to deliver training to its employees. The trainer is not responsible for the performance of the employees being trained, nor does he or she conduct their performance reviews. The trainer is generally not a member of the employees' work teams, department, unit, or division; he or she is a member of the HRD department responsible for training. Using HRD professionals who have never experienced the bumps and bruises of organizational life is part of the problem. HRD professionals usually are not integrated members of the organization. They may perform their duties with little regard for how their work affects the employees, the managers, and the organization. This is especially true when they are not responsible for the performance of their trainees or the impact that training has on the organization. They often train in a vacuum.

Organizations need to allow the players who have real-world experience to deliver training. We believe that managers are the ones who should be called up to bat. This is the only way the learning transfer will be successful. Organizations must use managers as partners in change. We believe that managers should be the champions of training rather than its gatekeepers.

## *Failure 5: Lack of a Performance Management System*

Many HRD professionals are frustrated with the lack of enthusiasm employees and managers have toward training and learning transfer. So instead of working to make certain that the transfer happens, they retreat to their classrooms, determined not to interfere. This contributes to the lack of learning transfer in organizations.

The biggest mistake HRD professionals make is their lack of vision. Many HRD professionals believe that training is the answer to all of the organization's ills. It isn't. Training can correct only those problems that are caused by the lack of knowledge or skill. Most of an organization's problems, however, are caused by the lack of a performance management system and by managerial malpractice.

In their book *Internal Consulting for HRD Professionals*, Jerry W. Gilley and Amy J. Coffern revealed that HRD professionals should be the ones responsible for developing and maintaining an organization-wide performance management system.[1] They should let go of their training responsibilities and allow managers to train their own employees. They should also focus their attention on improving organizational performance through internal consulting activities.

### Failure 6: Not Training the Right People for the Right Reasons

There are three myths of training that contribute to organizational failure. The first myth is that fixing employees' weaknesses will improve performance and enhance the organization's effectiveness. Almost all training activities are based on this premise. Sadly, this assumption is false. Fixing employees' weaknesses only makes their performance normal or average, not outstanding. Excellence can only be achieved by building on employees' strengths and managing their weaknesses, not through the elimination of weaknesses.

The second myth is that strengths will take care of themselves. If this were true, world-class athletes would never train. They would let their God-given talents and abilities propel them to

---

[1]J.W. Gilley and A.J. Coffern, *Internal Consulting for HRD Professionals: Tools, Techniques, and Strategies for Improving Organizational Performance* (Burr Ridge, IL: Irwin Professional Publishing, 1994), p. 57.

greatness. The reverse is true. The way you develop expertise is through practice, practice, practice, and practice. Training should be for the employees who already have exhibited a talent in a given area, not for someone who is only below average.

Third, many managers and employees believe that they can do anything they set their minds to. However, there are some things you just can't do regardless of how hard you try. Some managers live by the belief "If at first you don't succeed, try, try again," or "Practice makes perfect," or "If I can do it, you can do it." The problem with this logic is in the assumption that all people are the same, possessing an identical set of talents. We know that this is not true. People are different; we're not clones. We each have our own set of strengths.

### Failure 7:  Lack of Transfer of Learning

Another failure of today's HRD philosophy is that there is too much emphasis on the training event and not enough on the transfer of learning (see Figure 4.1). Training is only effective when the knowledge and skills taught are applied on the job. Performance improvement can't occur until employees apply what they learn. Training is not very useful unless it helps employees improve their performance, which, as a result, enhances organizational competitiveness.

One of the reasons transfer of learning fails is that most HRD professionals know little about it. This apparent lack of knowledge prevents them from discovering ways to improve learning transfer. It also makes HRD professionals reluctant to discuss transfer of learning strategies with managers and executives. Because of their inexperience, HRD professionals have little confidence in their ability to apply learning transfer strategies within the organization.

Employees tell us that the lack of immediate application to the job is one of the reasons learning fails to be transferred. Sometimes a delay of only two or three days will prevent learning transfer. A

**FIGURE 4.1**
*Five Phases of HRD*

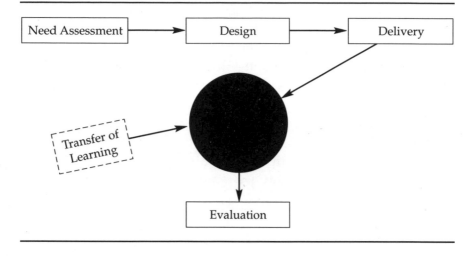

contributing factor is the lack of appropriateness and relevancy of a lot of the training they attend. Employees tell us that if it's not meaningful it's not used.

On other occasions, training is conducted too far in advance of its application so that when employees do have an opportunity to apply what they have learned they have forgotten a majority of it. Employees also tell us that peer pressure from co-workers prevents them from adopting new skills. Managers also contribute to the lack of learning transfer. Many managers don't perceive training as very important, so they don't allow their employees to participate. They also don't think employees have time for training, so it's not encouraged. If employees do attend training, many managers fail to reinforce what their employees have learned. We have even heard one manager tell his employees, "Forget that training stuff and get back to work." Some managers are threatened by the changes brought about through training. As a result, they interfere with the application of learning to the job in order to control the amount of change that occurs.

## CREATING A NEW HRD PHILOSOPHY

Too many organizations need a new HRD philosophy, one that addresses the real problems of the organization and focuses on improving organizational performance. The new HRD philosophy consists of seven major approaches:

1. Creating a training/business partnership.
2. Developing a results-oriented HRD strategy.
3. Improving the training delivery system so that skills can be acquired more easily and are better applied to the job.
4. Using managers as agents of change to help produce positive results.
5. Using HRD professionals as internal consultants responsible for developing performance management systems.
6. Identifying and developing employee strengths and managing weaknesses.
7. Developing learning transfer strategies that enhance organizational impact rather than focusing on training activity.

### Approach 1: Creating a Training/Business Partnership

The first step in creating a training/business partnership is for HRD professionals to fully understand the type of business their organization is in. This may require HRD professionals to participate in work-related activities that will enable them to appreciate and understand the business of their company. For example, Waste Management, one of the world's largest waste disposal companies, requires all their human resources and HRD professionals to spend three complete days in the field working alongside regular employees. This includes riding in garbage trucks hauling trash. Indeed, this participation will deepen HRD professionals' appreciation of the work of their organization.

The second step in creating a training/business partnership is to identify the business objectives of the organization. Executives and senior managers should be interviewed to provide their perspectives of the organization, its mission, strategic direction, problems, strengths, weaknesses, opportunities, constraints, goals and objectives, and financial position. This information should help HRD professionals determine the business objectives of the organization.

The third step in creating a partnership is for HRD professionals to examine their present training activities to determine if they help employees develop the needed skills to enhance organizational performance. Next, HRD professionals should determine if training will improve performance enough in order for the organization to reach its business objectives successfully. Finally, all future training programs should be developed to help the organization reach its objectives. Those programs that don't should never be offered to employees because they are a waste of time and money.

## Approach 2: Developing a Results-Oriented Training Strategy

The motto of an organization's training department should be "Results or Bust" because, without results, training isn't of much use to managers, employees, or the organization. It's easy to generate a lot of training activity and to advocate that it makes a difference, but it's much harder to identify the needed results and determine whether they were accomplished. It requires a total shift in emphasis. Training must produce specific outcomes on which the organization can rely to help it accomplish its business objectives. The new training strategy should be "training for impact" or "training for results." Both indicate an effort to accomplish something specific rather than training for training's sake.

## Approach 3: Improving the Training Delivery System

We discussed earlier the need for changing the way employees are trained. Traditional training has little impact on the behavioral changes organizations are so desperately seeking. HRD professionals need to get away from traditional training approaches and move to a modularized approach.

What is a modularized approach? Modularization is the breaking up of a training program into smaller units, or modules. Each module should last only a few hours. These modules can be delivered over several weeks. Therefore, the same amount of material can be covered with participants, but the learning period is expanded. In contrast, traditional training occurs in 8- to 16-hour sessions over a one- or two-day period. Participants must absorb, sort through, and figure out how to use all the knowledge and skills taught during a short period of time.

The benefits of the modularized approach over traditional training are many. First, participants can stay focused on the topic and not worry about what they are missing while at training, because they can return to work in a couple of hours. Second, participants can absorb and apply small bits of information much easier than complex and lengthy ones. Third, participants can practice the skills learned or apply the knowledge obtained between the training sessions. Fourth, participants can report back their applications of knowledge or use of skills at the beginning of each new session in order to get feedback from the facilitator or other participants. This will help reinforce learning and improve its transfer to the job.

One organization that has switched to the modularized approach is William M. Mercer Inc., the world's largest compensation, benefits, and human resources consulting firm. Mercer's management development program was previously a three-day course. The company changed it to six modules ranging in time from two hours to three-and-a-half hours and stretched it out over a 12-week period, with different management skills being discussed during each module. Between sessions, participants are asked to complete a work assignment that forces them to practice the skills they learned, and then they spend time reporting back to the group about their results. The results have been excellent. The participants enjoy the modularized approach and feel that they are developing useful skills they can use on the job.

## Approach 4:  Using Managers as Agents of Change

In Chapter Three, we discussed the advantages of using managers as trainers. We said that managers were the logical choice to provide technical training because they have technical expertise. Another reason managers should be used as trainers is that they are the ones responsible for developing employees. We also identified eight outcomes that can result when managers assume the training role. We will discuss these in more detail in Chapter Five.

## Approach 5:  Using HRD Professionals as Internal Consultants

In their book *Internal Consulting for HRD Professionals*,[2] Jerry W. Gilley and Amy J. Coffern discuss the eight purposes of internal consulting:  providing information, solving problems, conducting an effective diagnosis, providing recommendations, implementing change, building consensus and commitment, facilitating client learning, and improving organizational effectiveness. Gilley and Coffern believe that the first five purposes are the ones most frequently requested by clients and therefore refer to them as traditional purposes of internal consulting. The three remaining purposes are directly linked to improving organizational performance and require the most advanced skills of internal consultants.

We believe that the role of HRD professionals should evolve from the training role to that of internal consultant. In this role, they should support and supplement the efforts of managers by showing managers how to become competent trainers. HRD professionals should also provide managers with predesigned training programs that can be used in a modularized format.

However, as an internal consultant, the HRD professional's primary responsibility is to develop and maintain a performance management system within the organization. In order to create a performance management system, HRD internal consultants must:

---

[2] Ibid., pp. 8–14.

- Design and install an employee involvement system to encourage participation in performance management.
- Identify customer/client satisfaction measures to determine overall product/service satisfaction.
- Identify the competencies required for each job classification within the organization.
- Establish performance goals and objectives for operating units or divisions.
- Identify the principal outcomes or outputs produced by each job classification.
- Create competency maps that can be used as the foundation for training and development activities.
- Identify performance standards for each job classification.
- Develop performance measures.
- Create a performance evaluation system for each job classification using performance measures to compare actual performance with performance standards.
- Identify training and development strategies designed to close performance gaps discovered during performance evaluation.
- Develop performance feedback and reinforcement systems designed to foster performance improvement.
- Identify compensation and reward systems linked to performance improvement.

Once a performance management system has been established, it is the manager's responsibility to use it to improve employee performance.

### Approach 6: Identifying and Developing Strengths, Managing Weaknesses

One of the biggest mistakes managers make is trying to "fix" their employees rather than discovering the things that the employees can do very well. We believe that most training has been designed to fix weaknesses instead of capitalizing on employees' strengths. In Chapter Seven, we will discuss the process managers go through to develop areas of expertise that enable them to maximize personal productivity. Areas of expertise are based upon strengths, not weaknesses. So if a manager's or employee's areas of expertise produce the highest levels of performance, it makes sense to focus on them. Managers must develop their employees' strengths and manage their weaknesses.

Emmit Smith, All-Pro running back for the Dallas Cowboys, and Itzhak Perlman, world-renowned violinist, are team players, yet they are asked to perform from their areas of expertise and strength. Perlman is not asked to play the drums, nor is Smith asked to play defensive back. Why? Because it makes no sense to use such talented players in positions where they're not using their strengths to help the team. Why, then, do organizations spend millions of dollars every year on training that amounts to trying to fit round pegs into square holes? Let us repeat: Managers must focus on the strengths of their employees and build on them.

We will address the following discussion of strengths to you as a manager. If strengths are so important, how can you determine your strengths and those of your employees? Don Clifton and Paula Nelson, in their book *Sour with Your Strengths*, identified four characteristics that can be used in determining strengths:[3]

**Characteristic 1: Internal burning.**  Strengths start first in your mind as a burning desire to do something, for example, "I always wanted to be a manager," "I always wanted to coach football," or "I always wanted to be a musician." Your internal "self-talk" determines the things you are willing to try. What you tell yourself creates a pull or attraction toward one activity over another. This process begins early in life and over time begins to define who and what you are.

The mere desire for something does not determine that you have a strength in a given area, but it is the first clue that helps you determine if you're on track. For example, how many people do you know who want to be a manager for the sake of power,

---

[3]D.O. Clifton and P. Nelson, *Sour with Your Strengths* (New York: Delacorte Press, 1992), p. 43.

control, or career advancement? But how many of them demonstrate little concern for the development of people—the primary mission of management? We describe this as internal dishonesty, something that will derail you from identifying your true strengths and opportunities for mastery.

**Characteristic 2: Satisfaction high.**   When you complete a task or activity and receive high levels of satisfaction, you're focusing on a strength. A strength allows that you may get a kick out of doing something that you can't wait to do again. You receive intrinsic pleasure each time you perform that particular task. For example, as a manager do you delight in helping your employees grow and develop, improving their performance, examining their career options within the organization, teaching them a new way to do something? If the answer is yes to these, managing brings you satisfaction. Keep doing it. If the answer is no, self-select out of managing—find something else to do that brings you pleasure. Remember, not everyone is destined to be a manager!

Competencies and satisfactions are not always interrelated. You might be very good at doing something but hate doing it. For example, you may be good at getting results as a manager but hate working with people. Your competencies will not sustain you over the long haul. You will burn out because you lack satisfaction in the work you're doing. The key is, if it doesn't feel good, find something that does. Then you're practicing your strengths.

**Characteristic 3: Rapid learning.**   When something comes easy to you, or you learn it very quickly, it's an indication of a strength. You have heard of computer hackers. They are an excellent example of people who learn by jumping in and discovering how something is done. For them learning does not occur in a classroom but through interactions and experiences. This is what we mean by rapid learning. If you catch on quickly to something, you're likely to be good at it.

Continuous learning is a related indication of a strength. You want to learn as much as possible about things you're good at.

Reading this book is an example: You are trying to further develop your strengths as a manager. Otherwise, you would be doing something else with your time.

Slow learning, however, is evidence of a nonstrength. Some people just don't get it regardless of how hard they try. Several years ago, one of the authors (Gilley) tried to learn to ski. He tried and tried to master the simplest of techniques and just couldn't get it. Finally, after three different ski instructors quit trying to teach him how to ski, he reluctantly withdrew to the lounge. No strength, no learning, no mastery, no performance.

However, hitting a baseball is quite a different story. At the age of 40, this same author taught himself to switch-hit in less than three days. Now he is as good batting left-handed as he is right-handed. He has a strength in hitting a baseball but not in skiing. Rapid learning is an excellent way to determine whether or not you are using your strengths.

**Characteristic 4: The zone.**  When you perform a task or activity without any conscious awareness of the steps involved, we refer to it as the zone. The zone is a place where you produce a total performance of excellence. Everything happens just like clockwork. You perform unconsciously, relying on your strengths to carry you. It may be in giving a speech, writing a report, or making a presentation when you excel beyond your own expectations. You can't even explain how it happened, it just did. Reggie Jackson's three home runs in the last game of the 1977 World Series, Michael Jordan's 65-point explosion in the 1993 NBA semifinals, Mark Spitz's seven gold medals in the 1972 Olympic Games, and the University of Nebraska's fourth-quarter performance in the 1995 Orange Bowl, when they scored 16 points to win the NCAA National Championship, are all examples of individuals and teams performing in the zone, relying on their strengths. It's what champions and championships are made of.

The zone is the ultimate indication of a strength. It's the quality you need to build on. Positive experiences in the zone help build your self-esteem and shape your confidence. Both are needed to encourage you to perform again. You receive ultimate satisfaction while in the zone. You feel invincible, and you want to repeat the performance over and over again. With repetition comes improvement. For you as a manager, it is measured by the improved performance of your employees.

Nothing is more important in the reengineering of HRD than shifting the HRD philosophy from one focused on fixing weaknesses to one focused on building on strengths and managing weaknesses. We believe that your efforts will ensure the success of well-trained and well-developed employees. We will discuss your role as trainer in Chapter Six. Let's now look at the strategies you can use to build on strengths and manage weaknesses.

**Building on strengths.** The first step of building on strengths is for you and your employees to develop a personal master list of strengths. You can use the four characteristics previously discussed as a guide. Once a personal master list has been compiled, ask each of your employees to identify one strength he or she is willing to work on for a month. You should encourage your employees to select a strength that they have an opportunity to use on a daily basis. Ask each employee to use this strength as many times as possible during the month. Have employees keep a record of how they use their strength and the outcomes that occurred. Throughout the month you should informally discuss their efforts and provide encouragement and praise when appropriate. At the end of the month discuss with each employee how many times he or she was able to use the strength and what the outcomes were. Ask employees how they felt about using their strength and whether or not it helped them improve their performance.

The outcomes of this exercise could include improved performance, increased job satisfaction, enhanced working relationships, and increased confidence. This exercise should demonstrate to your employees that they have something special they can rely on to perform their duties. It should also demonstrate to you that employees don't mind improving performance if they are allowed to use their strengths rather than working on the things they can't do very well or are not interested in doing.

The next step is to repeat the process using another strength. You can repeat the process several times until all of the critical strengths have been further developed. The more complex the job, the longer this process will take.

As employees grow and develop, using their strengths to continuously improve their performance, there comes a time where each employee must pursue a career path that defines him or her within an organization. This might have been done prior to joining the organization through advanced training, graduate studies, and/or professional designation. Regardless, your employees must strike a direction and go for it. This decision should be made based on the total of their strengths. Through your career coaching role, you have an opportunity to assist your employees and to help counsel them during this decision-making period.

As your employees place their strengths into action, you must encourage them to continuously develop and improve their strengths. You should help them achieve mastery in their areas of strength through practice, practice, and more practice, just as professional quarterbacks practice throwing the football over and over again throughout their career in the NFL. In short, mastery comes about through thousands of hours of hard work.

Finally, employees can relive their successes in order to enjoy them over and over again. In fact, the more you relive past successes, the more you are inviting success in the future. Employees, teams, and organizations are never stronger than when they have their successes clearly pictured in their mind. We think there are three things you and your employees can do to build on your strengths: visualize them, write about them, and talk about them.

Visualizing success is a process by which you mentally rehearse an event. Over and over again, you picture yourself giving a speech, writing a report, completing a calculation, or making a presentation. Whatever it is you do well, visualize it. This mental rehearsal allows you to relive all the emotions and satisfactions of the moment. Each time you relive the event, it inspires you to further develop your strengths.

You can also relive a successful event by writing about it. You can write down a full description characterizing the strength: where the event took place, what it felt like to succeed, your greatest moment, and the dialogue that took place throughout. Be as creative as possible, but be realistic. Once you have written about the event, reread your account over and over until it's fresh in your mind, as though you were experiencing it again. The goal is to inspire yourself to further develop the strengths that lead you to be successful.

Many of us need to tell someone about our successes. We encourage those of you who are interactive learners to talk about how you successfully used a strength. You should discuss what your proudest moments were and how your strengths helped you accomplish your victory. Talk about the heroes you would like to emulate and how you compare with them. This will give you a target to shoot for and inspire you to work even harder to be as good as they are.

**Managing weaknesses.** Identifying weaknesses is the first step to managing them. Weaknesses are easier to spot than strengths because we are used to thinking in terms of weakness. For example, others have been pointing your weaknesses out to you most of your life. Your teachers, parents, supervisors, managers, and even your spouse have been telling you the things you don't do well. In fact, some of us have a hard time finding good things about ourselves or others because negative criticism is the prevalent mode of thought. However, when you do need to identify weaknesses, there are some behavioral clues that might help.

Slow learning on the part of your employees is the first indication of a weakness.[4] A closely related behavior is that your

---

[4]Ibid., p. 79.

employees don't profit from repeating an experience. In other words, they don't show any growth after several months of doing a task. They do just enough to function, just enough to hang in there, but they lack the ability to achieve excellence. When they have a weakness, employees don't think about improving their performance. Their only concern is to get through the day.

Weakness can be demonstrated when your employees have to consciously think about the steps of a process. This is normal when an employee is first learning a new job, but it is not normal after several months of experience. Employees who have the talent to do a particular job can complete the tasks involved without thinking about them; the tasks become subconscious.

Employees who have a weakness often become defensive about their performance. They feel inferior about not performing up to standards and are prepared to attack anyone who says anything to them. Some employees become obsessive over a weakness in an attempt to overcome it. This addictive behavior overtakes them, and they become overly focused on their performance. These employees may work excessive hours in order to compensate for their weaknesses. They simply don't know how to let go of the behavior. The obsession becomes destructive, and ultimately such employees will burn out or you will have to let them go. In any case, you must guard against this type of negative behavior and act quickly when you observe it.

Some employees pay a high psychological price for their weaknesses. Instead of admitting to them, they allow themselves to be placed in situations where they fail over and over again. The result of this cycle is a reduction in their self-esteem. Over time, it will produce a negative self-concept and then these employees will have little or no confidence in their abilities. Without confidence, employees cannot perform to your expectations. An increase in sick days, loss of interest and motivation, and an increase in the excuses for their performance will be the result.

Identifying a weakness is only the first step. You must figure out how to help your employees manage their weaknesses. This includes four strategies: delegating, partnering, preventing, and alternatives.[5]

Delegating is one of the best ways to manage your employees' weaknesses. Your job is to find someone in the organization who possesses a strength in an area where there is a weakness. For example, several years ago we discovered that we didn't have very strong talent for managing paperwork in our office. In fact, it was a weakness that caused us some embarrassment. So we delegated the task of managing the paperwork to our assistant, Donna. She was an outstanding organizer. She also enjoyed doing it and welcomed the challenge. She made us all look good. It was also an excellent development process for her as well. By handling the paper flow, she came to understand our jobs better. It helped her move more quickly inside the organization.

Partnering is not what you may think—the matching of one person's strengths to another person's weakness. Rather, it is the teaming of strengths—combining two employees' strengths together to achieve a goal. They can do a better job together than they can separately. For example, one person does the selling while the other handles customer service because those are their respective strengths. Another example would be that one person does the classroom training while his or her partner does the instructional design work. Complementary strengths overcome weaknesses every time.

When you teach your employees not to allow themselves to be put in situations in which they will consistently fail you are doing what is known as *preventing*. Your employees must discover what they don't do well and stop doing it. You must be willing to support their decisions. You must encourage your employees to find things they're good at and let them work on those. For example, while at William M. Mercer, we discovered that some employees were very good at gathering information and preparing it for

---

[5]Ibid., p. 90.

computer analysis but were not very good at analyzing and making recommendations to our consultants, while there were employees with the opposite talents—a perfect opportunity to combine partnering and preventing. We simply had the employees who were good at data gathering and preparing work on those tasks, and the employees who were good at analysis and recommendations work on those. The result was that strengths and strengths worked together instead of half strength and half weakness.

Alternatives are different ways of accomplishing the same tasks. Accepting alternatives requires you to be willing to live with difference. In fact, the "other" way may even be better. Some of the best quality improvement and performance efficiencies have been discovered when managers encourage their employees to find an alternative way to get a job done. Remember, encourage your employees to use alternatives that build on their strengths.

### Approach 7: Overcoming the Transfer of Learning Blues

You are the key to overcoming the transfer of learning blues. That's right, you are. Why? You're the only person in the organization truly responsible for performance improvement. We understand that executives are responsible for the profitability of the organization and, therefore, are accountable for the quality and efficiency of the organization. But most executives have not got a clue how to make it happen. Only the frontline soldiers really know how the war is being fought. As a manager, you are the person who works daily to improve production, performance, and quality. You must shoulder the responsibility for training your employees and making certain they use the skills taught on the job. Then and only then will organizational performance improve.

You must overcome the primary barrier of learning transfer, which is *you*. Your attitude toward training is of paramount importance. If you believe in training, you'll reinforce new learning, you won't interfere with new and different ways of improving performance, and you'll create an environment supportive of training. As a supporter of training, you'll work to improve your employees' attitudes and perceptions about training, you'll help your employees overcome their discomfort with change, and you'll work to make certain that training is relevant and practical. As the champion of training, you'll make certain that your employees work together to reinforce change and help each other improve their performance. Finally, you become an active agent for change by accepting your role as trainer. As trainer, one of your responsibilities is to help your employees prepare for change. You must help them see change as a positive opportunity rather than as a threat. To do this, you must encourage your employees to examine their present performance, determine their strengths and weaknesses, and develop a plan that will allow them to build on their strengths while managing their weaknesses. In other words, you must motivate your employees to become responsible for their own learning. If they own it, they will support it.

Managing change also includes making certain that training is conducted immediately before application. Training that is timely will help employees transfer the learning. Employees learn best when training is problem focused, allowing them to face the problem (previous performance) and apply possible solutions (training). This will ensure application.

You must also communicate the importance of training to your employees. This will help you answer the question employees almost always ask: "What's in it for me?" You can also let them know how much you support the training they are participating in. This will enhance their willingness to try new skills. You, however, must be patient with your employees as they try to acquire new skills and knowledge, particularly if performance dips as they struggle to integrate new skills and knowledge on the job. Your patience will help foster a supportive work environment and encourage employees to take some risks in improving their performance.

You should find ways of rewarding and recognizing your employees for acquiring new skills and knowledge. This will reinforce the changes they are making. The more positive the experience is, the more likely it is that they will embrace change in the future.

In Chapter Six, we will examine the training role in greater detail. We will look at how managers can make the transition to trainer and discuss how critical this transition is in order for you to become a performance coach. We will also examine several transfer-of-learning strategies that you can use after training to ensure that your employees apply what they learn. They include:

- Refresher courses.
- Journals and daily logs.
- Training and performance aids.
- Assignments and follow-up activities.
- Failure analysis.

By developing positive relationships with your employees, adopting the four roles of a performance coach, creating self-directed and self-confident employees, and rewarding your employees for their efforts, you will be a more successful manager. However, an appropriate HRD philosophy, one that supports and encourages improved organizational performance, must be in place. We believe that by avoiding or overcoming the seven failures outlined in this chapter, you will produce the organizational results you need.

*Chapter Five*

# Building Employee Relationships that Enhance Commitment

*The Performance Coaching Process*

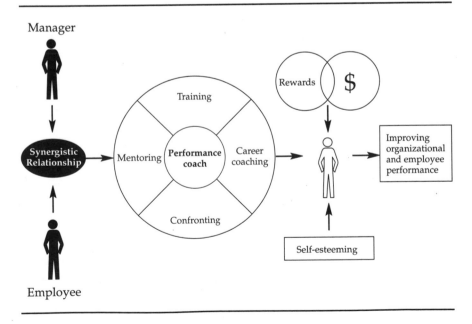

Manager

Employee

Synergistic Relationship

Training

Mentoring

Performance coach

Career coaching

Confronting

Rewards $

Improving organizational and employee performance

Self-esteeming

Relationships are critical to the development of each and every one of us both inside and outside the work setting. How individuals function within an organization is based primarily on the written and unwritten rules. The rules can take on a variety of forms—they can be in a human resource manual, on posters on the walls, or even in "off-the-record" communications from a more experienced employee. As a new employee tries to assimilate into the work culture, it takes him or her time to understand the values, behaviors, and beliefs of the organization. He or she tries to develop relationships with co-workers and superiors, which is usually difficult because the new employee doesn't know whether the relationship is healthy. New employees have to intuitively accept the rules of the organization while feeling through the labyrinth of individual egos. What makes for a healthy and functioning relationship? Does the employee–manager relationship need to have open and honest communications, or are employees supposed to read between the lines?

Why is it important to have healthy relationships in an organization? There are five reasons. Having healthy relationships:

1. Enhances and builds managers' and employees' self-esteem.
2. Enhances productivity.
3. Enhances and builds organizational communication.
4. Enhances and builds organizational understanding.
5. Enhances and builds organizational commitment.

We feel there are nine critical components to healthy functioning relationships. They are as follows: freedom from fear, communication, interaction, acceptance, personal involvement, trust, honesty, self-esteem, and professional development (see Figure 5.1). How did we decide on these nine components? In interviews with executives and managers we asked, "What characteristics would be ideal in your relationships with your clients or customers?" They have constantly mentioned these nine basic components as the most fundamental and needed attributes for healthy relationships. We asked if these components exist in their personal relationships and they have responded with a resounding "Yes." Where the

**FIGURE 5.1**
*Relationship Model*

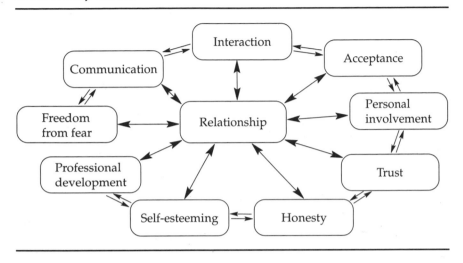

model breaks down is in dealing with their employee relationships. However, most executives and managers we have interviewed believe that these nine components are fundamental to their success as a performance coach. Later in this chapter, we will provide a detailed description of each component and how to use the relationship model on the job.

Notice in Figure 5.1 that each of the nine components has arrows going to and from the relationship circle. The most critical part of this model is that each component has a reciprocal relationship with the inner circle. Furthermore, the components also interact with each other, allowing reciprocity to exist within each component relationship. To clearly describe the model, we must first define and discuss each component independently.

## FREEDOM FROM FEAR

Fear kills organizational as well as individual performance. We have consistently heard employees say they are unwilling to invest in relationship building because their boss intimidates them or because they are afraid of reprisals. We have to eliminate fear from organizations, but first let's define the four characteristics of fear:

Frustration

Ego

Anger

Resentment or Rage

When employees become frustrated with a situation or a relationship, they begin to fear whether they made the right decision. This can negatively impact their ego. As the frustration builds, employees begin to realize that they have no control over the outcome. This means that their productivity decreases proportionately to their frustration level. As the frustration level increases, a "disruptive ego" starts to take control of the communication process, and anger and resentment build.

Fear is the root of anger. Anger allows the fear to exist because the root emotion, fear, is never appropriately addressed. Thus, you begin losing faith in the process and in the relationship. It is easier to become angry than to feel uncomfortable. As a result, one of two things happens when anger gets to a boiling point: You either erupt into a rage and say things you would normally not say, or you hold the anger in and let it turn into resentment. Resentment is then intrinsically nurtured, and the relationship may never be repaired.

A perfect example of fear destroying a relationship is when a manager we worked with delegated a specific task to a subordinate. The subordinate was very excited about successfully completing the job but was fearful because he did not know exactly what the manager wanted—the manager did not clearly define the task that was to be completed. The employee kept asking the manager for advice, and this caused the manager to become fearful that maybe she should not have delegated the task. As the fear increased, so did the manager's frustration, which culminated in a verbal exchange with the employee. The manager then apologized to the employee, but the damage was already done. The manager ended up finishing the task but carried a resentment about the capabilities of the employee. Since fear existed in their relationship, the parties were unable to create a win–win situation.

How do we eliminate fear in relationships? For fear to be eliminated, you must first create a work environment that is safe from emotional, verbal, and physical abuse. If any of these exist, the relationship is dysfunctional and neither managers nor employees will grow, develop, or become creative. One of the greatest benefits of a fear-free relationship is that both you and your employees are allowed to think outside the box. To think outside the box means to expand our knowledge by creatively thinking of solutions that are outside of our personal life experiences or frame of reference. If fear exists, all your employees are forced to think alike, which stifles the growth of the organization.

Managers know the greatest resource in their organization is its people. Then why don't managers create fear-free relationships? The answer is simple. Senior executives too often are fearful of the upcoming stars in the organization, and instead of creating positive relationships they say things like, "That was the way I was treated," or "It has always been done that way." That is like saying, "Since I was physically abused by my parents, I have the right to do the same to my children." Is that right? We think not. We believe that creating fear in any relationship is damaging to the growth and development of employees and the organization.

The goal of a fearless relationship is to allow you and your employees to grow, develop, and think outside the box. In other words, creativity flourishes when fear is eliminated. In addition, in fear-free environments your employees are challenged and stimulated to solve complex problems, thus allowing both you and themselves the opportunity to build a positive relationship that benefits the organization.

## COMMUNICATION

Once the work environment has become free of fear, the next step is for you to improve the communication process. Too often the communication process breaks down because the message is somewhat distorted. How is the process distorted? First, the employee sending the message does not construct the message in a cohesive and understandable fashion. In a classic true story of miscommunication, a flight attendant realized that the right engine of the aircraft was on fire. She called the cockpit and told the pilot, who quickly shut off the right engine. The plane crashed and burned. What happened? The flight attendant and the pilot were facing different directions so that the right engine for the flight attendant was the left engine for the pilot. Does this kind of miscommunication occur in your organization? Probably, but maybe in a more subtle fashion.

Managers are usually guilty of conducting one-way communication, and they expect employees to agree without any discourse. Many employees will always say, "Yes I can do that," even when they know they may not be able to complete the assignment. Instead of talking it through with the manager, they just make an attempt at completing the task and end up failing. You must take the time to clearly define the communication channels and how to best use them so that your employees know exactly what is being said.

Clear communication can be accomplished through an agreement of all employees as how to effectively communicate with each other. Whether they use face-to-face contact, telephone, memo, voice mail, or even e-mail, managers must develop a common language based on a similar understanding of signs and symbols. One of the biggest mistakes organizations make is that they train only the senior management. As a result, senior managers develop a language of their own, and then expect the rest of the members of the organization to understand what they are talking about even without a frame of reference. Organizations must take the time to teach everyone the ins and outs of the way information is communicated.

Having the same frame of reference allows for a two-way relationship between manager and employee because both can use a similar language. However, if managers have poor listening skills, the two-way communication process is ineffective. Managers must take on the responsibility of listening and successfully comprehending messages from their employees. The following 10 steps will lead to good listening:

1. Maintain eye contact.
2. Nod frequently and say things like "OK," "Ahh haa," or "Mmmm."
3. Sit in a nonthreatening environment (e.g., in a conference room, not behind your desk).
4. Stop working.
5. Do not look at your watch.
6. Do not look restless or fidget.
7. Do not cross your arms or legs.
8. Put your phone on call forwarding or voice mail and if it rings, ignore it.
9. Do not talk over or interrupt the other person.
10. Do not let other people interrupt your conversation.

If you are guilty of violating more than three of the steps listed above, you are a very poor listener, which means that your employees most likely do not feel comfortable talking with you. Here is a quick and easy exercise to help you improve your listening skills. Make a list each time you catch yourself listening poorly. If you are honest with yourself, you will start to see a pattern, and once you are aware of the problem you can correct it.

The hardest part in changing behavior is taking the time to introspect. Forcing yourself to think about your efforts can help you identify the things you need to improve. Once you have developed good listening skills, you can focus on reciprocal or two-way communication. If you are focused on sending and receiving messages, providing appropriate feedback, and challenging your employees to think outside the box, you have a greater opportunity to create a stimulating work environment. For relationships to prosper, communication must not only be reciprocal, it must also be open. Relationships where employees feel they can speak their mind without fear of repercussions on the job can only be accomplished if the work environment is free of fear. The ideal environment is one where open, two-way communication exists and healthy relationships flourish.

## INTERACTION

If you are truly to have fear-free and healthy communication in your relationships with employees, you must also allow for interaction. As the information age evolves, many managers forget about the importance of personal interaction with their employees. In the past, managers have used memos to avoid interacting and building relationships. With the onslaught of e-mail and voice mail, managers can avoid face-to-face meetings with their employees altogether. This is a very scary thought.

If you forget the importance of physically and emotionally interacting with your employees, the organization as a whole becomes less responsive and more reactive. When you keep playing telephone tag and/or never interact, emotional commitment to your employees will never be developed because there is no personal involvement at stake. This will have a negative impact on organizations.

Several years ago we observed a senior management team use e-mail and voice mail instead of face-to-face interaction to announce a major downsizing. Why? The reason was that it was quicker and more convenient—management could avoid a serious confrontation. Are we that afraid of each other that we can't pass on bad as well as good news to those with whom we have relationships? We sure hope not. But if you believe this is acceptable behavior, you may as well stop reading this book now, because interaction is absolutely critical to building healthy relationships.

## ACCEPTANCE

For relationships to have acceptance it is critical that they be nonjudgmental. This is not to say that relationships cannot be insightful, or that those involved will be limited to talking about unimportant or trivial issues. Acceptance means not judging the thoughts and ideas of your employees, and not being too quick to draw conclusions or make inferences. If employees feel that they have to defend everything they are saying, they will only say the things that are safe.

Brainstorming provides an excellent example of the importance of acceptance. One of the rules of brainstorming is that anything goes, but that no one is allowed to shoot down another person's idea. Occasionally a participant in a brainstorming group will make a negative comment about an idea or a participant will say, "That's a stupid idea." The individual who shared the initial idea will usually withdraw and will be afraid to say anything else because of the negative repercussions. Instead of the group being highly motivated and stimulated to think outside the box, the members are forced to wear blinders in order to protect themselves. This narrows the creative solutions of the group.

Do you know how Campbell's Chunky Style Soup was developed? A group of employees was brainstorming on how to develop a new line of soups. One of the employees stated, "A soup should be able to be eaten with a fork." None of the other employees criticized the statement; instead they ran with the idea, which eventually became part of the promotional tag line that Campbell's used for the product.

The following rules should be stated at the beginning of a brainstorming session should be applied in creating an accepting relationship:

1. Anything that is said will be respected and accepted.
2. Do not comment negatively about any statement or idea.
3. Listen to the complete thought.
4. Do not interrupt.
5. Allow time for processing or integration.

To accept others means using these rules whether you are interacting with 1 employee or 10. Using these rules will allow employees to express themselves without fear. Remember that everyone has a unique frame of reference for life, and that as managers it is extremely important that you take the time to identify your employees' values. By doing this you will protect yourself from making inappropriate comments that could be construed as judgmental.

How do you find out the values of your employees? By asking questions and observing behavior. By identifying what is important to each of your employees, you create an environment that will foster healthy communication and interaction. By knowing your employees' values, you will know which buttons to push to motivate them based on their frame of reference, not yours. If you have 10 employees to manage, you may need to use a different strategy to motivate each employee. If you have taken the time to ask questions and observe behavior, you will know which comments will improve and which ones will be detrimental to the relationship.

If you are seen as someone who is accepting and willing to take the time to listen attentively to the needs of all your employees, your employees will feel extremely comfortable in their relationship with you.

## PERSONAL INVOLVEMENT

The next step in building a healthy relationship is to become personally involved with your employees. Getting personal can be very difficult for some managers because they feel that knowing their employees' personal history is inappropriate. We disagree. We believe that people coach people and that the more personally involved you are with your employees, the better you can coach them.

Personal involvement means taking the time to get to know your employees as people. However, employees must be willing to let you get to know them. The boundaries are set by you and your employees. Thus, you must be very careful to ask appropriate questions. When thinking about boundaries, keep in mind that you should never ask a question that you would feel uncomfortable in answering. Also, remember that the way you say certain things will have an impact on how comfortable your employees feel about answering them.

The easiest way for you to get personally involved with employees is for your employees to see that you are more than just a manager. They need to know that you are also a human being. Show your employees that you have interests outside of work. These interests may be sports, hobbies, your family, and so on. If you open the door to disclosing yourself, your employees will know that it is all right for them to do the same. Being personal is √ critical to the development of a deeper relationship; without it the relationship can only be superficial.

## TRUST

The sixth component of the relationship model is trust. Trust can only be truly established if the relationship has become personal. Once trust is grounded in your relationship with your employees you both will feel safe in what is said between you. If trust is nonexistent, your employees will not reveal important information to you. In other words, for trust to work, a degree of confidentiality must exist. If you are perceived as untrustworthy and/or as a gossip, it will be very difficult for you to build any trusting relationships with your employees. For example, if an employee tells you that he or she is having difficulty working with another employee, and you turn around and tell the other person without first discussing it with the original person, you will have destroyed your confidentiality with both employees and jeopardized your respective relationship.

What can you do when you need to discuss an issue that is confidential? Remember that you have a responsibility to the organization, so here are some suggestions:

1. Ask the employee what he or she would do if your roles were reversed.
2. Never discuss the comments of the employee without permission.

3. Explain why you are doing what you are doing.
4. Get buy-in or agreement before you proceed.

For trust to be an integral part of relationship development, it must be based on truth. Truth is fundamental to trust. Truth implies open and direct communication. As a result, hidden agendas are avoided and discouraged, and employees are encouraged to be forthright.

Respect is also critical to trust. Respect is needed to develop a healthy relationship, because without respect for each other the trust level will be much lower. Respect requires you to listen actively to the problems and needs of your employees.

Trust also means sharing information. The personal dimension of the relationship will determine the type and level of the information shared. Trust therefore ensures truthful disclosure, reciprocal sharing, and attentive listening skills.

By maintaining confidentiality, truth, respect, and sharing in your employee relationships, you will be able to develop a more concise and synergistic set of interactions. Trust must have a strong relationship with confidentiality. This is critical for the existence of a dynamic, growing, and maturing relationship. Keep in mind that you will be getting into a much deeper interaction with your employees than before. In the earlier parts of the relationship you were learning about each other, about each other's boundaries, and how the interaction would occur. Now you can take the relationship to a much deeper, more involved level.

## HONESTY

The next component after trust is honesty. A relationship without honesty is a relationship destined for disaster. Why? Simply put, if the manager or employee is dishonest, one or both individuals will lose. The goal of any relationship is to create a win–win situation. When dishonesty is present between managers and employees, their relationship will be based on fear. This is not to say that sometimes you don't hold back some information that could hurt your employees, but what you do tell them must always be the truth. We observed a manager who told the members of his team point-blank that a new member was hired at the same job classification as the rest of the team, when in reality the person was hired at a higher level. This means that the manager blatantly lied or at the very least stretched the truth. As the team members began finding out the truth, their relationship with the manager began to deteriorate. First, the team members lost a great deal of respect for their manager. Second, they did not confront their manager but they became extremely judgmental with regard to any of the work he assigned. As a result, the team members began to interact less and less with their manager. When they had to communicate, they communicated with him in a very direct way, answering questions very formally, giving only yes–no answers, and giving only the information that was asked for, no more, no less. The team members became disillusioned and fear set in among them. They came to have extreme doubt in their relationship with the manager and grew fearful in their once-healthy relationship with fellow teammates. Some members maintained honesty and trust with their teammates so their relationship remained positive, yet other relationships became strained. In these relationships, trust vanished and backstabbing occurred as team members tried to align themselves with the manager.

The relationship within the team has improved over time, but the members are still very disillusioned with the manager. They collectively have lost respect for him and feel he is not credible. Some individuals now are questioning whether they will stay in the department, and others are thinking about leaving the organization. In this real-life situation, one lie has destroyed or severely damaged over a dozen relationships.

What should the manager have done to prevent this disaster? The manager should have examined the rationale for his hiring decision and how the new employee's role would be different from that of the other team members. At the very least the manager should have explained the differing career path of each team member.

Honesty is the best policy. As managers, it is critical that you understand the ramifications of any comment you make. Even though it may be difficult for you to have confrontations with employees, it's better than the other possible outcomes. It is usually quite clear what could or will happen.

When honesty exists in a relationship, it allows managers and employees the opportunity to discuss issues that are well outside the box. In an honest relationship, employees feel very good about their role within the organization. They also feel good about their work. This increases their self-esteem, and as a result productivity increases. Your employees feel good about interacting with you and they feel that they can talk to you about a variety of topics that will benefit the organization.

## SELF-ESTEEMING

When thinking of improving the self-esteem of your employees, you have to first understand how to feel about yourself. Instead of focusing on all the things that you cannot do, focus on the things you can do. You must recognize those things at which you excel, things that make you feel intrinsically satisfied. Since most people spend time beating themselves up, let's do a quick exercise that will allow you to focus on your good points. Make a list of all the things at which you excel, both at work and outside of work. The list may look like this:

1. I am friendly.
2. I am honest.
3. I am intelligent.
4. I work well on teams.
5. I am a hard worker.
6. I am kind.
7. I am empathetic.
8. I am a good athlete.
9. I am competitive.
10. I am disciplined.

Once you have completed the list, ask yourself if you truly believe everything you wrote. Review the list again and remove those items you don't really believe are true. Add any new items at this time. The attribute list most likely shows that you are a very valuable manager to your organization and to people outside of work.

The next step in the exercise is to ask some people you value inside and outside of the organization to list the things at which they believe you excel. This will most likely let you see that others think highly of you as well. Keep both lists somewhere accessible, because to build other people's self-esteem you must first truly believe in yourself.

Once you believe in yourself, the next step in building self-esteem is to accept who you are. Some of us are tall or short, blonde or brunette, extroverted or introverted, and so on. By accepting who you are you can challenge yourself to build healthier relationships with people who will enhance your self-esteem.

After you have accepted who you are and truly believe in yourself, you are able to build self-esteeming relationships with your employees. What does self-esteeming mean? Self-esteeming is the culmination of all the other components of the relationship model (i.e., freedom from fear, honesty, and the rest). If you are missing any one component it will be very difficult to build self-esteeming relationships.

Self-esteeming comes when managers and employees reciprocally build each other's self-esteem as they move toward mutually desired results. How can both individuals increase their self-esteem at the same time? It's easy. Because managers understand what is important to their employees on an intrinsic level, they select motivational strategies that challenge and stimulate their employees, thus creating a higher level of trust and honesty, which in turn increases the employees' confidence.

Obviously, as confidence increases, self-esteem increases. This may sounds a lot like empowerment, but self-esteeming is a two-way process while empowerment is one-way. In empowerment, the manager still maintains control but gives it to the employees.

This is where growth and development stop. Self-esteeming takes the relationship to a much deeper level. In return for receiving some control, the employee must now challenge and stimulate the manager with regard to his or her role and responsibility, which will create a higher level of confidence for the manager. This allows reciprocal self-esteem, or self-esteeming, to occur.

When a relationship becomes self-esteeming it becomes synergistic. The end result of the relationship is much bigger, greater, and deeper than either the manager or the employee could have ever imagined. This is the unleashed power that can result if you take the risk as a manager and build self-esteeming relationships. Now that your relationship has gotten to a synergistic point through self-esteeming, you can now focus on the professional and personal development of each of your employees.

## PERSONAL AND PROFESSIONAL DEVELOPMENT

The final component of the relationship model is personal and professional development. After the relationship has become self-esteeming, it's time to develop each of your employees personally and professionally. As we discussed in the self-esteeming dimension, managers and employees have equal control over their respective development. The employee must take responsibility for creating a developmental plan. No one knows better what an employee's goals, desires, achievements, and abilities are than the employee. If your employees depend on you to tell them what direction they need to head, then they're in deep trouble.

If an employee's value structure is the same as yours, then great—but how often does this really happen? Not often, because everyone's experiences and perceptions of the world are different. Therefore, you must consider the personal values of each of your employees. If values are not considered, you may end up trying to force round pegs into square holes.

We observed a situation where not considering the values of an employee became a serious problem. The manager felt that the employee was very much like she was and assumed that they both shared the same values. The manager assumed the employee's values included being driven, being hard working, and wanting to climb to the top of the corporate ladder. The manager and the employee had built a relatively healthy relationship. They could talk about anything job-related and even things about each other's private life. They respected each other and were able to trust each other, but the manager did not ask the necessary questions that would enable her to give the employee work assignments that would advance the employee's career. As a result, the manager gave the employee several work assignments based on her own values, not the employee's. The employee's performance on those assignments was less than satisfactory, which seriously jeopardized their once-healthy relationship. What kinds of questions should be asked to help you discover the career goals and values of an employee? The 10 questions you should consider asking are the following:

1. What kind of work are you currently doing?
2. What do you like and dislike about this kind of work?
3. What other kind of work or project would you like to be involved in?
4. What characteristics do you feel are critical for success within the organization?
5. What characteristics do you feel are detrimental to success within the organization?
6. What kind of training do you need to be successful?
7. What areas do you need development in?
8. What do you feel are your greatest strengths?
9. What is your perfect or ideal job description?
10. Where do you see yourself in one, three, and five years?

These questions are all open-ended, requiring the employee to be open and honest in discussing the relevant issues of his or her own career. As the previous example illustrates, the manager made the wrong decision by not asking these questions and by assuming she knew what was best for the employee.

Who needs to be honest? The employee must come clean at this point to protect his career because of the assumptions his manager is making. Once he is honest with his manager about his personal values, the manager will better understand the employee and his developmental needs, thus allowing the relationship to get to a deeper level of self-esteeming. The Developmental Plan (Figure 5.2) will allow your employees to find a way to create a living, breathing plan of action that you both can use.

## APPLYING THE RELATIONSHIP MODEL

Now that we have defined for you each component of the relationship model, we would like to explain how easy it is to use. The first step is to identify where you are working with each of your employees. Remember that each employee relationship is different and therefore you can be at different components of the relationship model with different employees. Once you have identified where you are, then you keep working in a forward direction (follow the arrows on the diagram) until you reach the personal and professional development component.

What do you do if something comes up and the relationship deteriorates? First, examine why the relationship has deteriorated. This should tell you where you are on the relationship model. Once you have identified where you are on the relationship model, you must make adjustments. For example, if your relationship had progressed to the trust component, and a problem developed that caused the relationship to fall to the interaction component, you have to change your behavior to meet the needs of the interaction component. Once you have rebuilt the relationship at that level, you cannot immediately progress forward to the trust component. Instead, the relationship must go through each of the intervening components (i.e., acceptance and personal) to be reenergized.

**FIGURE 5.2**
*Development Plan*

|  | Behavioral Needs (Assertive, interpersonal, etc.) | Developmental Needs (Presentation, prospecting, etc.) | Technological Needs (Computer, etc.) |
|---|---|---|---|
| One-year plan |  |  |  |
| Three-year plan |  |  |  |
| Five-year plan |  |  |  |

**Directions:** In each plan fill out your personal forecast as to where you want to be, that is, what kind of role and responsibility you want in the organization. The boxes on the right explain how you are going to improve yourself to obtain your desired results.

As this example demonstrates, using the model is a simple process. The goal of the relationship model is to build self-esteeming relationships that are synergistic and challenging for both you and your employees. Once this is accomplished you can begin to focus on becoming a successful performance coach by working within the four roles we discuss in the upcoming chapters.

*Chapter Six*

# The Manager as Trainer

*The Performance Coaching Process*

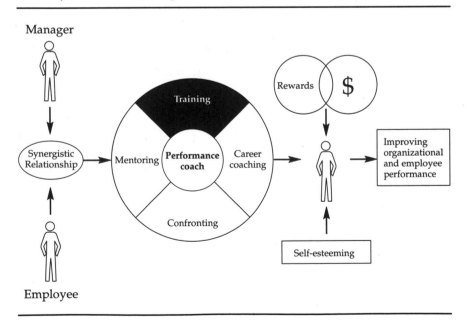

In Chapter Five, we discussed the importance of building a synergistic relationship between you and your employees, and its impact on the organization. The next phase of the performance coaching process is to identify and discuss the four roles of a performance coach: trainer, career coach, confronter, and mentor. We want to begin our journey by examining the role of trainer.

## WHO SHOULD BE RESPONSIBLE FOR TRAINING?

In many organizations, the training responsibility is delegated to professional trainers who are skilled in learning theory, program design, and delivery. Should this be the case? In order to answer this question, let's look at the purpose of training to see if this helps us determine who should be responsible for training.

The purpose of training is to increase employees' knowledge, skills, or competencies so that they can perform their jobs better. In addition, training programs should be designed to meet the performance needs of the organization. Therefore, the individuals responsible for training are ultimately responsible for improving employee performance and organizational productivity. Who in the organization is in position to accomplish this objective? Are professional trainers truly accountable for employee performance? Are they asked to explain why productivity decreases? Does the organization hold professional trainers accountable for such developments? The answer is no! Whom do they hold accountable for performance and productivity? Managers.

Because professional trainers are not truly responsible for employee performance and organizational productivity, the responsibility should fall at the feet of managers. Therefore, training should become the responsibility of managers because they are the only organizational players truly held accountable for employee performance and organizational productivity.

## THE EVOLUTION OF PROFESSIONAL TRAINERS TO INTERNAL CONSULTANTS

Professional trainers have another serious problem. They are often not perceived as credible within the organization. This is because many senior managers view professional trainers merely as teachers. Such a perception is supported because professional trainers rarely produce any direct revenue for the organization. As a result, short-term-oriented senior managers have a difficult time seeing how professional trainers' overall contributions improve the organization and help it remain competitive. This causes many organizational leaders to view professional trainers as outside the organizational mainstream, or as mere overhead. This often limits their effectiveness within an organization.

If managers become responsible for training, what should professional trainers do in the organization? Some organizations may attempt to rid themselves of these individuals because of their perceived lack of credibility and value. However, this would be a serious mistake. Professional trainers often have had their fingers on the pulse of the organization for years but haven't been allowed to function as agents of change. Organizations have an excellent opportunity to use professional trainers as more than just a delivery mechanism. They can give professional trainers an active role in developing and implementing new and creative changes throughout the organization by using them properly, that is, as internal consultants.

As internal consultants, professional trainers can perform a wide range of activities for organizations. In Chapter Four, we outlined one of their fundamental responsibilities, which is to design, develop, and maintain performance management systems within the organization. This type of activity can have a significant impact on the effectiveness of the organization. It can help managers produce the performance improvements they need to keep the organization competitive.

In addition, professional trainers could function as process consultants. As process consultants, they can help the organization address specific performance problems, paying attention to how things are done rather than to the tasks that are performed. During this activity, internal consultants must examine the organizational structure, analyze job design and work flow, evaluate the performance appraisal system, examine employee attitudes, identify performance criteria and standards, and develop quality process improvement procedures. The primary goal of this activity is to improve organizational effectiveness. This activity is often referred to as *change consulting*.

Professional trainers have also developed skills and competencies to help them identify and implement change. They can be used in providing information, solving performance problems, conducting effective diagnosis, providing recommendations, implementing change, building consensus and commitment, facilitating client learning, and improving organizational effectiveness (see Figure 6.1). These eight activities make up the hierarchy of purpose for internal consultants.[1] The first five purposes are the ones most frequently requested by the organization. They are often referred to as traditional purposes of consulting. The three remaining purposes require the most advanced skills of internal consultants, which include understanding the consulting process as well as establishing and managing the consultant/client relationship.

### The Training Partnership

Professional trainers should forge a partnership with managers in their efforts to improve employee performance and organization productivity. The training partnership includes training managers to become trainers, designing and developing training activities that bring about real change, and team teaching with managers during training activities.

---

[1]A.N. Turner, "Consulting is More than Giving Advice," *Harvard Business Review* 61(5), 1983, pp. 120–129.

**FIGURE 6.1**
*Internal Consultant's Hierarchy of Purpose*

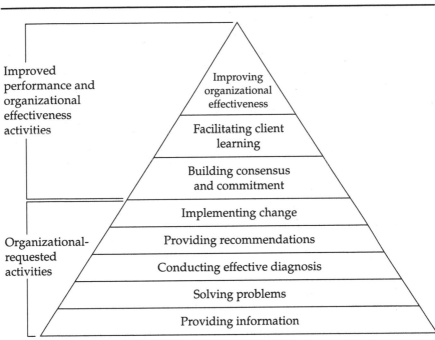

Adapted by permission of the *Harvard Business Review*. An exhibit from "Consulting is More than Giving Advice" by Arthur N. Turner (September/October 1983) Copyright © 1983 by the President and Fellows of Harvard College; All Rights Reseverd.

Professional trainers should be responsible for teaching managers how to train others. This is a very important activity for professional trainers to perform because it can help managers become competent as trainers, which can have a significant impact on the organization and the employees. Such training includes lessons on presentation and facilitation skills, how to answer questions, and how to lead group discussions.

Professional trainers should also be responsible for designing and developing training activities. Managers are not qualified to function as instructional designers. They need professional trainers to design and develop training activities that will help them improve employees' performance and organizational productivity.

There will be times when it is appropriate for professional trainers to team-teach a training program with managers. This most often occurs in very specialized training or advanced training. New innovations, technology, and complex skills may also require the expertise of a professional trainer. When this approach is required, professional trainers should be used to conduct classroom training while managers supplement their employees' learning. On the job, managers should be actively reinforcing what their employees have learned and be available to provide feedback and support while their employees struggle to apply what they have learned.

## WHAT IS TRAINING ANYWAY?

The focus of training is to help employees improve and develop knowledge, skills, or competencies for their current jobs. Training can be conducted in both formal and informal learning settings, which include on-the-job activities. The delivery systems used in training can include computer-based training, interactive video, instructor-led training, satellite programs, employee self-directed learning, and on-the-job training.

When training, the primary activity of managers is classroom instruction. This includes formal training activities as well as on-the-job training, whether unstructured (informal) or structured (formal). Unstructured on-the-job training activities are those conducted daily in organizations: A manager provides simple job-related information in an informal and matter-of-fact manner. For example, as they work together, a manager gives a new employee of a fast-food restaurant information on how to greet customers. Such information is not required by the organization as a part of formal training but is based on the insight and experience of the supervisor. It may or may not be given to all employees because it occurs during a spur-of-the-moment sharing activity as a way of helping the new employee learn one of the tricks of the trade. On the other hand, structured on-the-job training activities are offered to all employees equally in order to provide continuity among employees. These activities are designed to provide the correct or exact procedures for conducting a particular job. They are very detailed and require many hours to complete. They are considered structured because there is a proper order required and they are often sequenced with other training activities. Such formal training should include learning objectives and activities designed to bring about appropriate behaviors, skills, or competencies. To provide realism and to improve learning transfer, structured on-the-job training often is conducted at the work station or job site. This gives employees a chance to practice job skills and provides immediate feedback on performance.

## MANAGERS AS TRAINERS

Managers as trainers—what a concept. Many organizations are already using this approach in such areas as sales training. Companies like Hewlett Packard, AT&T, and Merrill Lynch, to name a few, successfully train their sales forces with proven sales leaders from within the organization. Grady Floyd, district sales manager for Hewlett Packard Medical Group, is responsible for sales training. He feels the reason for his success is that he understands the business and lives it on a daily basis. Even though someone outside of the sales department designs the training program, Floyd is responsible for delivering it. Floyd feels that because he has 25 years of experience in the field, the participants respect him and his expertise. He is successful because he has credibility with the employees attending the program. Perhaps professional trainers could do a better, more polished presentation, but they lack the firsthand experience needed to make them credible.

AT&T's senior international sales training consultant, Cheri MacManus, feels that her success as a salesperson has allowed her to be successful as a trainer. She understands the sales process, and she can identify problems when they occur by answering questions and providing examples that employees understand.

Some questions may arise here. Why does the managers-as-trainers concept usually stop at sales training? Why not use the same idea and let the most qualified person train his or her own employees? Why not let the managers be responsible for all the training of their employees? The primary reason given today is that the professional trainers are afraid to give up training. They're frightened that the organization will not need them anymore. However, professional trainers do have a significant role to play in the organization. As we stated earlier, they should become internal consultants responsible for performance management systems and thereby bring about organizational change.

## BECOMING A TRAINER

Managers should follow four important principles when training their employees. First, present new information only if it is meaningful and practical. If theory is introduced, it should be linked with a practical application. This approach should reduce any resistance to learning theoretical material.

Second, present information in a manner that permits mastery. Employees maintain the ability to learn throughout their lifetime. In fact, many studies document that the ability to learn only diminishes slightly until the age of 55, and then continues to diminish at only a very moderate rate.

Third, present only one idea or concept at a time—to help employees integrate it with their existing knowledge. Remember, the goal of training is the development of knowledge, skills, or competencies that will help employees improve their performance. Therefore, the issue is not how much information is shared or how rigorous the training process is, but simply the development of the desired knowledge, skills, or competencies.

Fourth, use feedback and frequent summaries to facilitate and foster retention and recall. Because of the lack of time for training, these activities are often overlooked or greatly deemphasized. Failure to use feedback and summaries in training could result in incorrect application of the material or a failure to apply it on the job.

## THE SEVEN LAWS OF TRAINING

Training is a professional field. Like any other professional field, it has laws that guide its practitioners. Such laws combine to create a process in which specific individuals and definite activities produce specific results.

Essentially, training is a communication process between you and your employees designed to develop their knowledge, skills, and competencies in order for them to produce a desired outcome or result. Training, in the simplest sense, occurs through the communication of experiences. Experiences can take several forms, such as using a specific skill to complete a task or executing a correct procedure to produce a desired outcome or result.

For managers, training is a process of breaking down complicated tasks, skills, and/or competencies into small steps and communicating them to less experienced individuals (employees). These employees, then, learn the tasks, skills, and competencies one step at a time. If training is successful, the employees being trained will be able to perform the tasks, skills, and/or competencies proficiently. When training is applied, performance and productivity should improve.

Of course, training is a very complex undertaking that requires great skill and expertise. In order for managers to master the role of trainer, they must incorporate seven distinct elements into each training activity:

- Two people—a trainer and a learner (employee).

- Two mental factors—a common language or medium of communication and the tasks, skills, or competencies to be communicated.

- Three activities—delivery by the trainer; learning by the employee; and review and application of tasks, skills, and competencies by the employee on the job.[2]

---

[2]J.W. Gilley and S.A. Eggkand, Principles of Human Resource Development (Reading, MA: Addison-Wesley, 1988), pp. 29–30.

Each of these should be present regardless of the length of the training session. They combine to make up the *training–learning process*.

In order to make certain that these seven elements are properly blended, seven laws of training should be followed. If each of these laws is present, the training–learning process will be complete. Absence of any one of them may result in your employees failing to learn. These laws are designed to help you perform successfully in your role as trainer.

### 1. The Law of the Manager

*A manager–trainer must be the person who has knowledge of and experience with the task, skill, or competency being taught.*

This law may seem too obvious even to consider, yet many managers violate it. The words *knowledge* and *experience* are the cornerstone of this law. A manager's knowledge and experience are the material with which he or she works, and without either there is no training. Having an inexperienced manager act as trainer would be like the blind trying to lead the blind. Competent and experienced managers give their employees needed confidence. In the same way, a well-prepared manager awakens in his or her employees the desire to learn.

But the law of the manager goes deeper still. A manager (trainer) who only half knows a task, skill, or competency is likely to be lifeless and cold, while one who fully understands it will likely be fired with enthusiasm. This knowledge combined with enthusiasm will unconsciously inspire employees' interest.

Still, it is not enough to possess great knowledge. You must also have the ability to inspire employees with a love of learning. We refer to this ability as a "passion" for training, and it is very contagious. Only with a passionate trainer will employees become independent and truly self-directed.

**Rules for the manager–trainer.**  To ensure that you don't violate the law of the manager, you should follow several rules.

Each will help you master the art of training and foster interest and desire on the part of your employees:

1. Prepare for each training session by fresh study and review.

2. Illustrate new ideas and facts in terms of everyday experiences of your employees. In other words, provide a familiar frame of reference for employees by presenting new information in terms and symbols they can understand.

3. Discover the "natural order" of material or information to be presented. In every training program there is a natural path from the simplest ideas and steps to the most complex. Material must be presented in this fashion in order to ensure understanding.

4. Relate the material to the lives of your employees.

5. Set aside a definite time for study for each training session, in advance of the instruction. This will help you gather fresh insights, interest, and illustrations prior to the actual performance.

6. Use as many training aids as possible to reinforce learning.

7. Avoid overloading your employees with all you know about a topic or skill. The mastery of a few ideas or skills is better than an ineffective smattering of many.

8. Allow employees to practice and apply what they have learned.[3]

**Violations and mistakes.**   Discussion of the law of the manager would be incomplete without some mention of the frequent violations. Even the very best trainer may spoil his or her most careful and detailed work by thoughtless blunders. Being aware of some common violations and mistakes will help you minimize errors and maintain credibility. They include the following:

1. The very ignorance of your employees regarding the subject may tempt you to neglect careful preparation and study.

---

[3]Ibid., p. 35.

2. Many mangers maintain that it is their employees' responsibility, not theirs, to study. This type of indifference and lack of preparation will ultimately lead to habits that will seriously hamper the effectiveness of the training.

3. Many managers who have not mastered the material believe that they can make it through a training session with random talk and an occasional story. Some even fill the time with unrelated exercises or videotapes.

4. Many managers attempt to hide their lack of knowledge or preparation by presenting material in a manner beyond the comprehension of their employees.

These are just a sample of violations and mistakes made by a few managers who fail to prepare adequately for training activities. Many managers also lack the communication skills and enthusiasm necessary to inspire their employees to learn.


## 2. The Law of the Learner

*A learner (employee) is the person who participates in the training program. Learners must focus their attention on the task, skill, or competency being taught.*

By *attention* we mean directing the mind on some object. It may be external, as when the learner watches carefully the operation of a machine or assembly procedures; or it may be internal, as when the learner reflects on the meaning of some idea or recalls some past experience. There are three types of attention present in learning situations: passive attention, active attention, and secondary passive attention. Each is important from the point of view of the training and learning.

*Passive attention* is an instinctive, basic type of attention. Someone using this type of attention is not really concentrating but rather simply following the strongest stimulus present. Passive attention involves no effort, because the learner is letting the forces around him or her control the thinking process. For example, most people use passive attention when they're watching television or listening to the radio. In training, this type of attention is common.

Managers must guard against it, because it can have very negative effects—the most serious one being inadequate learning. This occurs because the learners (employees) have little interest in remembering the information being shared; and because their concentration is not very focused, they fail to remember most if not all of what the managers (trainers) share with them.

*Active attention,* a distinctively human type of attention, requires employees to distinguish separate stimuli and select consciously only the appropriate ones. For example, when you're working at your desk and your telephone rings, you can select between two stimuli, your work or the telephone. You will respond to whichever of the two stimuli is the strongest or most appropriate. Regardless, you become actively involved in that stimulus, and your concentration is fixed.

In training, active attention is present during activities that require participants to be involved. Demonstrations, simulations, role playing, and group discussions are commonly used to enhance and focus participants' concentration. Your employees will remember much more information or master skills easier when active attention is being used, but it requires tremendous energy. As a result, your employees may experience mental overload if active attention is used for a long period of time. It is, however, very appropriate to use active attention when critical information or complicated skills are being taught.

*Secondary passive attention* is similar to passive attention in that the subject or object is so attractive and interesting in and of itself that it demands little or no effort to study it. However, it is different from passive attention because the learner is focused on the material and is persistent in his or her efforts to understand and comprehend it. Generally speaking, employees learn best and most easily when they are absorbed in their work. Under this condition, learning is so fascinating that it simply carries the employees along with it.

In training, you can use a variety of methods to help produce secondary passive attention. The most common ones are games, exercises, case studies, and Outward Bound–type activities. Each of these methods uses a diversion (i.e., a game) to focus the employees' attention away from the main learning objective, which allows them to be drawn into the activity. In other words, employees don't realize that they're engaged in a learning activity. While participating in the activity, your employees, however, are learning and applying the very task, skill, or competency that you want them to master.

Successful employee performance such as winning the game or identifying the correct responses to a case study is not the objective of the activity. What is important is that your employees gain the insights, skills, or knowledge you're trying to teach. Secondary passive attention enables this to happen without the normal resistance associated with learning a new task, skill, or competency.

It is obvious that the attention most desirable to cultivate is the secondary passive type. It allows employees to have a pleasant and effective learning experience while improving their learning. The implication is that training must be presented in such a way as to motivate interest.

Trainers and training materials may be full of vital and essential information, but it is of little value if your employees are not paying attention or concentrating. They will never be able to apply what they learn unless they fully understand how to correctly use a task, skill, or competency. Employees must work with a fixed purpose—in other words, they must think.

There are two primary hindrances to attention: apathy and distraction. Each of these must be addressed by you in order to minimize their effects. Apathy refers to the lack of interest in a subject or skill, perhaps because of a bad training experience in the past or the learner's poor self-confidence. Distraction is when your employees' attention is divided among a variety of stimuli. In classroom training, two or more conversations going on at the same time is a form of a distraction. Under this condition your responsibility is to isolate the negative or unproductive stimuli and neutralize them.

**Rules for the manager–trainer.**  To avoid violating the law of the learner, you should follow several rules:

1. Never begin a training session until the active attention of your employees has been secured.

2. Pause whenever the attention is interrupted or lost, and wait until it is completely regained before starting.

3. Never completely exhaust the attention of your employees.

4. Adapt the length of the exercise to the ages and physical conditions of your employees.

5. Appeal whenever possible to the personal interests of your employees.

6. Use a variety of instructional methods to arouse the attention of your employees.

7. Identify sources of distraction and reduce them to a minimum.

8. Make the presentation as attractive as possible, using illustrations, graphics, and training aids.

9. Use third-party stories, dialogue, and analogies whenever possible to illustrate the point.

10. Maintain and exhibit a genuine interest in the subject or skill through fresh study and review.

11. Prepare before the session several thought-provoking questions.

12. Maintain appropriate eye contact with your employees, and use appropriate voice inflection and body language.[4]

**Violations and mistakes.**    Many managers violate the law of the learner by failing to gain the attention of their employees prior to beginning a training session. They might as well start before their employees have entered the room, or continue after they have left. Some continue after their employees' power of attention has been exhausted and when fatigue has set in. Others kill the power of attention by failing to utilize fresh inquiries or new ideas and illustrations. Some even enter the training environment with old notes and materials that immediately turn off their employees.

---

[4]Ibid., p. 36–45.

Perhaps the worst mistake comes when trainers make little or no attempt to discover the interests and prior experiences of the employees, thus often presenting material employees already understand. In such cases, boredom sets in and a negative attitude develops toward both the trainer and the training.

### 3. The Law of the Language

*The language used as a medium between the trainer and the learner must be common to both.*

Language has been called the vehicle of thought. It is made up of words and symbols whose meaning is based on common experiences and understandings. Training is not complete unless it is expressed in plain and intelligent language common to the trainees. This means that your explanations should be in their language, and not mere repetitions of the ready-made definitions of someone else. In some training this is extremely important because much of the information is highly technical, and the terminology involved can be a language unto itself. Managers who must present technical material should know the technical language.

**Rules for the manager–trainer.**  As with laws 1 and 2, you should also follow several rules for the law of the language:

1. Use the simplest and fewest words that will express the desired meaning.
2. Carefully and constantly study the language of your employees.
3. Frequently test your employees' understanding of key words to make certain that they are not being incorrectly used.
4. Use short sentences of simple construction.
5. Use illustrations to help your employees understand the meaning of words and symbols.
6. If your employees fail to understand, repeat the idea or thought using other words, or use an analogy or example.
7. Identify the terms, symbols, and language that employees are familiar with prior to the training session, and adjust your communications accordingly.

8. Encourage your employees to communicate during training. This will help you determine the level of their understanding as well as identify specific words used.

**Violations and mistakes.**   Many managers have no proper appreciation of the wonderful character and complexity of language; they simply take language for granted. Also, fooled by the employees who look interested, they may assume that their listeners thoroughly understand when in reality they do not. The misuse of language is another common violation. Many trainers never attempt to determine if they are using the words or symbols correctly.

Many employees do not ask for explanations or examples, and trainers therefore assume that the employees understand the information or skill. But just because employees have not asked questions it may not be time to move forward. A lack of questions could indicate that employees are seriously confused. Managers should test for understanding prior to moving forward.

Some employees may be entertained by the manager's training style but may fail to hear what he or she has to say. It is also possible to look directly at a person while being somewhere else mentally. There may be a more pressing matter at home or at work that is occupying your employees' attention. It is your responsibility to determine if this is the case and to find ways to minimize the distraction.

### 4. The Law of the Training Session

*The task, skill, or competency to be learned must be explained in a way that employees can comprehend it.*

Another way to express the law of the training session is: The unknown must be explained by means of the known. All training activities must begin somewhere. If the subject is completely new, then identify a point at which to begin, one that closely associates the material to something the employee is familiar with. This could be an experience, a related topic, or a procedure or process; it could even be an example or story that provides a common framework from which to build the training activity.

All training activities should be based on an identified set of learning objectives. Once the objectives and experiences are determined, the trainer should prioritize and sequence them in an appropriate order to properly link one fact or concept to another, remembering that simple and concrete ideas lead naturally to general and abstract ideas. Employees must master each step fully before beginning the next. If not, they may find themselves proceeding into unknown areas without proper preparation.

In order to ensure employees' comprehension, the trainer must share information in a way that links the unknown to the known. Unless the trainer follows this approach, communication is impossible.

**Rules for the manager–trainer.**   Several rules apply to the law of the training session that help foster its application:

1. Discover what your employees know of the task, skill, or competency; this is the starting point.
2. Utilize your employees' knowledge and experience.
3. Relate every session—as much as possible—to former sessions as well as to the experience of your employees.
4. Arrange the presentation so that each step of the program leads easily and naturally to the next.
5. Use illustrations your employees can identify with.
6. Encourage your employees to make use of their own knowledge.
7. Choose the problems you assign to your employees from their own work activities and/or interests.
8. Encourage your employees to find illustrations from their own experiences and share them with their fellow employees.

**Violations and mistakes.**   It is not unusual for managers to allow their employees to participate in training activities they are inadequately prepared for. This can create a great deal of frustration and stress for your employees; it can also result in their failure to meet to learning objectives, which can negatively impact their self-esteem. More important, it can cause bad feelings toward you and toward training.

Too many times managers fail to thoroughly familiarize employees with elementary facts and definitions. They incorrectly assume a certain level of knowledge or skill, which causes them to begin training at an inappropriate point of entry. If this occurs, employees may not be able to understand the information being presented because they lack prerequisite knowledge or experience. As a result, a learning opportunity will be missed, which could affect all future learning.

Another common error is the failure to connect the present material with previous material. Many employees cannot make the connection between different tasks and skills on their own. They often view various sections of presented material as *separate*, because there is no attempt to integrate them. In addition, the material being presented is often not connected to the material yet to come. This creates problems for future applications and relationships.

Many managers fail to motivate their employees by not fostering an attitude of discovery. Thus, they create a situation in which employees fail to pay attention and miss many opportunities to grow and develop. Managers also present too much material, which impedes their employees' ability to understand and apply the information. They also provide too little time for practice and mastery of complex skills or competencies.

In many cases, every step of a task, skill, or competency is not always thoroughly understood before the next is attempted. Thus, employees get frustrated and confused, which can prevent them from learning the correct way of performing. You should delay presenting a new step until your employees have demonstrated that they have mastered the previous one. Otherwise, the result will be inadequate understanding and development.

## 5. The Law of the Training Process

*The training process must be arousing and exciting; it must stimulate the employee's mind to grasp the desired thought or to master the desired task, skill, or competency.*

It is often believed that training cannot take place without a trainer. This is, of course, not the case. People can learn without a trainer. In fact, true teaching does not "give knowledge" but rather stimulates employees to gain knowledge for themselves. In other words, you might say that those who teach best are those who teach least.

Since the employee's primary aim in training is to acquire knowledge, to develop skills and competencies, or to change behaviors—or all three—it could be said that employees who are taught without having to do any studying for themselves will be like those who are fed without being given any chance to exercise: They will lose both their appetite and their strength. Thus, if growth and development are to occur, the responsibility of learning should shift from you to your employee.

You, however, must provide the material or information in such a manner that it motivates your employees to become absorbed by it. Anything less will result in inadequate preparation, development, and growth. You must stimulate your employees' minds and challenge their abilities and skills. Only then can your employees become truly self-directed.

**Rules for the manager–trainer.**    Like the other laws, the law of the training process suggests some practical rules for instruction:

1.  Adapt information, materials, and/or assignments to the ages, experience, preparation, and skills of your employees.
2.  Consider carefully the information, material, and/ or assignment to be presented, and identify its points of contact with the lives, interests, and experiences of your employees.

3. Excite your employees' interest in the information, material, and/or assignment through statements of inquiry or thought-provoking questions.
4. Consider it your principal responsibility to awaken the minds of your employees, and, not rest until each employee demonstrates his or her mental activity and involvement.
5. Place yourself frequently in the position of your employees and join in their search for additional information and knowledge.
6. Repress your impatience with your employees' inability to grasp concepts or to master skills.
7. Allow employees to sort out the material and gain understanding.
8. Repress the desire to tell all you know or think about the subject or skill.
9. Encourage employees to ask questions when they are confused or puzzled.
10. Allow your employees the time to answer questions or to complete exercises on their own.
11. Be dedicated to beginning each training session in a manner that stirs your employees' interests and involvement.

**Violations and mistakes.** Many managers neglect these rules, which often kills employees' interest and enthusiasm for training. Managers may then wonder why employees are not motivated and excited about training. Some trainers have an inappropriate and impatient attitude toward their employees regarding their abilities, skills, and level of comprehension. Others criticize their employees' lack of memory. Still others have an overdemanding attitude toward employees.

The result of impatient training is that your employees comprehend only enough to be able to perform at an entry level instead of thoroughly learning and understanding the material, which could greatly improve their performance. Thus, true learning is negated or never obtained.

### 6. The Law of the Learning Process

*The learning process is complete when the employees can apply what they have learned to the job.*

It should be pointed out that learning is not memorization and repetition of the words and ideas of the manager. Employees should strive for a deeper understanding of the memorized words by applying the newly learned task, skill, or competency to the job. In fact, the learning process is not complete until employees can apply what they learn. You and your employees must constantly direct your efforts to accomplishing this purpose.

**Rules for the manager–trainer.** The rules that follow from the law of the learning process are useful for employees as well as for managers:

1. Help your employees form a clear idea of the work to be done.
2. Ask your employees to express in words or in writing the meaning of the training session as they understand it.
3. Answer your employees' questions in a nonthreatening manner.
4. Strive to make your employees self-directed and independent investigators.
5. Seek constantly to develop in your employees a profound regard for truth as something noble and enduring.

**Violations and mistakes.** The most common violations and mistakes of training occur as a result of not understanding the learning process. They are perhaps the most fatal of all, since each one may result in the loss of learning. The first mistake is the trainer's failure to insist on original thinking by the employees. Second, practical applications are persistently neglected. Third, many employees are left in the dark because the training lacks a well-thought-out set of instructions or directions. In many cases, employees fail to question the manager or training material. They blindly assume that they are correct and accurate. This can cause serious difficulties when the employees attempt to apply what they have learned to the job.

### 7. The Law of Review, Application, and Evaluation

*Employees must have the opportunity to review, rethink, apply, and evaluate the tasks, skills, and competencies they have learned.*

This law seeks to ensure that the employees fully understand what they have learned and how it can be used on the job.

A review is more than a repetition. A machine may repeat a process, but only an intelligent human being can review it. Review implies the rethinking of a task, skill, or competency for the purpose of deepening the employee's understanding of how to perform it correctly. This includes making new associations and conceptualizing.

A review is not a separate event added to the instructional process but rather an important part of the process itself. It is an essential condition of good training. Not to review is to leave the work half done. Any exercise or activity that uses previously presented information or material is considered a review. One of the best and most practical forms of review is to pose some realistic problem or circumstance and give employees the opportunity to apply the new task, skill, or competency to the problem or circumstance. Such a contrived situation is safer and more secure than an actual situation on the job, and it allows for mistakes that otherwise may cost the organization thousands of dollars.

The final activity the trainer must perform is evaluation, both program and learner. The ultimate purpose of evaluation is to determine the impact that training has on the employee as well as the organization. This includes the design and development of valid and reliable tests and measurements.

There are four types of training evaluations, each of which has a different purpose. *Reaction* evaluations are designed to determine participants' feelings and attitudes toward training. *Learning* evaluations, both pretest and posttests, measure learning. *Behavior* evaluations determine the changes in employee behavior or performance action. A fourth type of evaluation is called a *result* or *impact* evaluation. This is designed to determine the ultimate outcomes of training for both the employees and the organization.

Behavior and result evaluations are best used when the cost of training is high and there is a way to measure the change in behavior and/or quantify the results. Reaction and learning evaluations are best when training costs are low and it is important to determine the emotional responses of learners or determine if learning occurred. Both are easy to develop and manage compared to the behavior and results evaluations. Each of the four types has its place in the evaluation scheme, and it is the trainer's responsibility to decide when one would be more appropriate than another.

**Rules for the manager–trainer.**   Consider the following rules for the law of review, application, and evaluation:

1. Realize that review is a part of the instruction process.
2. Establish a set time for review.
3. Get into the habit of providing a review at the completion of each training session as well as after each section or at the close of a topic or subject.
4. Integrate old material into new material.
5. Never omit a final review.
6. Seek comprehensive and complete groupings of material.
7. Identify as many applications as possible.
8. Demand that employees rethink and regroup material and information in order to make personal applications.
9. Identify the outcomes of training and select an appropriate evaluation scheme.

**Violations and mistakes.**   The most obvious violation of this law is to totally neglect the review, application, and evaluation process. Such neglect is a sign of a poor manager–trainer. The second most common error is to conduct an inadequate review. This is often the result of an impatient or hurried manager who is more concerned with getting through the material than with enabling his or her employees to grow and develop.

Another mistake is to delay all reviews until the end of the program when most of the information, material, or ideas may have been largely forgotten. In this circumstance, the review is simply an example of poor relearning with little interest or value to employees. Still another mistake is to make the review merely a lifeless restatement of the previous facts, ideas, and information provided earlier in the training program.

One of the biggest mistakes managers make is to rely exclusively on reaction evaluation to determine the success of training. The main reason they do is that reaction evaluations are easy to design and administer. However, trainers need to use learning, behavior, and result evaluations to provide a complete picture of how training positively or negatively affects performance. These other evaluations could also indicate that training had little or no impact on performance.

## USING TRANSFER OF LEARNING STRATEGIES TO IMPROVE PERFORMANCE

Managers must accept the responsibility for learning transfer, but they must also understand the importance of developing work environments that embrace the success of learning transfer. The first step is to provide an environment that is conducive to learning, one that is free of distractions, interruptions, and barriers.

Many managers expect employees to apply new skills and knowledge immediately; however, the reality is that such behavior cannot and will not occur easily. It takes a great deal of practice for new skills to be developed and a great deal of discipline to integrate new knowledge. Therefore, employees must be prepared for a period when it may appear that training was a waste of time. You can be a great help by coaching employees on how difficult it is to transfer new skills and knowledge to the job.

There are several strategies you can use to help your employees transfer learning to the job. Each strategy helps employees reinforce previous learning, practice new skills, and integrate new knowledge. They include the use of refresher courses, journals and daily logs, training and performance aids, follow-up activities, and failure analysis.[5]

### Refresher Courses

An effective activity managers can offer after training is a short refresher course for employees. During refresher courses employees can (1) identify barriers that prevent learning transfer, (2) talk about the difficulties they are having integrating the new skill or knowledge in the workplace, (3) share how they have incorporated the new skill or knowledge in their particular situation, and (4) get reinforcement of the major learning points of the training program.

The type of dialogue found in refresher courses may greatly enhance transfer because it allows employees to learn from each other. They can find strategies that are successful, as well as talk about things that prevent the transfer of learning. It also gives the manager an opportunity to reemphasize the key points of training by reminding employees of their importance and application. These sessions should be fairly short, perhaps one to three hours, but not more than a half day.

### Journals and Daily Logs

You can help your employees develop journals and daily logs designed to capture their progress in the development of new skills and knowledge. Such activities allow employees to document the circumstances and events surrounding the application of specific skills or integration of knowledge. Employees should describe the circumstances and events in as much detail as possible. They should also describe the outcomes of the application or integration. Over time, journals and daily logs will show the circumstances and events that enhance learning transfer, and those that do not.

---

[5]J.W. Gilley and A.J. Coffen, Internal Consulting for HRD Professionals: Tools, Techniques and Strategies for Improving Organizational Performance (Burr Ridge, IL: Irwin Professional Publishing, 1994), pp. 84–90.

Journals can be used to describe complex events that require greater detail and documentation. Journals also allow employees to tell a story about their growth and development efforts. Employees often use journals to capture personal dialogue and conversations that would be inappropriate to share with others.

Daily logs are a form of "personal contracting," which encourages employees to record their daily progress. Managers can use these logs to identify the barriers within the organization that prevent learning transfer. In addition, daily logs serve as a constant reminder of the importance of the new skill and knowledge acquired and their application to the workplace.

### Training and Performance Aids

As a manager, you should provide training or performance aids that allow new skills and knowledge to be applied more easily. Such aids should be designed in a user-friendly and practical manner. The goal of these tools should be to help employees keep key points fresh in their minds throughout their daily work schedule. They can be small laminated cards, Post-it notes with key words, posters, and so on. You should discuss these tools at the end of the regular training program and demonstrate how to use them. Also, in refresher courses you can hand them out as a way of reminding employees of the key points of training. At the very least, you should discuss how the tools can help your employees in their quest to transfer skills and knowledge to the job.

### Follow-Up Activities

You can also aid the transfer of learning by giving proper and prompt follow-up activities, such as one-on-one interviews, which identify the successes and difficulties your employees are having. While it may be impossible to follow up with all of your employees, it is important to choose a sample of individuals for follow-up sessions. These sessions can be similar to focus groups. Individual and group follow-up sessions can also help you redesign the training program, because they give you critical information about the success or failure of learning activities and the application of the course content.

### Failure Analysis

Because new skills and knowledge may interfere with current employee performance, it is critical that you analyze the long-term effects of such a conflict and determine their impact on overall productivity. We call this failure analysis. Failure analysis is designed to help you better identify possible conflicts so that you can better integrate learning in the future.

The interference that occurs when employees attempt to integrate new skills or knowledge often confuses them. This can cause productivity to slip for a short time while a new skill or idea is being infused into the day-to-day behavior of employees. You may get nervous about the loss of productivity and be reluctant to continue supporting the acquisition of new skills and knowledge. However, failure is part of the learning process and growth of each employee. Failure is a healthy by-product of job growth, and a fear-free relationship can provide an opportunity for learning to occur. Failure does not equal disaster. What you're looking for are the *reasons* why learning transfer did not produce the desired or hoped-for results.

One suggestion is to allow employees to try out new skills or knowledge in safe environments such as work simulations and case studies. Employees who fail in such comfortable and supportive settings will learn a great deal about their current skill set and what will or will not work on the job. Learning failure often allows for a quicker, more accurate application of new skills and knowledge. Short-term gains are substituted for long-term success. Learning failure helps employees increase their long-term productivity and improves their overall job performance.

### *Employee Responsibilities*

You have the responsibility to communicate to your employees that they are ultimately responsible for the transfer of learning. To allow learning transfer, employees must have the desire to manage themselves and the work environment. This level of self-discipline is not present in all employees, which is the reason transfer of learning does not occur for everyone.

As a performance coach, you must understand the importance and significance of your role in the transfer of learning. You must clearly communicate the importance of new skills and knowledge in improving employee performance and organizational productivity.

*Chapter Seven*

# The Manager as Career Coach

## The Performance Coaching Process

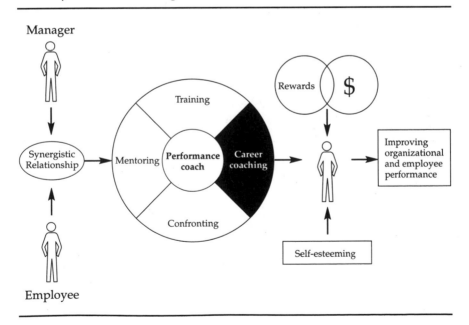

Within the organization, the employee is responsible for career planning while the organization is responsible for career management. Because of this separation of responsibilities, organizations tend to take two approaches when establishing career planning and development programs. They either employ career counseling specialists or relinquish the responsibility directly to managers.

Using managers as career coaches appeals to many organizations. It allows the individual most familiar with an employee's performance to recommend strategies to help the employee make career decisions. Using managers can be cheaper than using a separate career counseling staff. Using managers also makes sense because managers are already being held accountable for employee performance and should be motivated to help improve, develop, and promote their employees. Finally, managers are in a unique position to motivate and encourage their employees, and career coaching provides them this opportunity.

Managers serious about improving performance and quality must accept the role of career coach. As a career coach, your primary responsibility would be to help your employees examine their career options, explore alternatives, and identify their future career path. You should also help employees analyze their skills, interests, and abilities. Such information will help the organization match its needs with those of its employees.

## ORGANIZATIONAL BENEFITS OF CAREER COACHING

Career coaching promotes overall organizational performance through better allocation of human resources. In other words, you can help your organization by getting the right person in the right job. Your efforts will help protect the organization from investing too much time and money in employees who are not suited for specific jobs and responsibilities.

Another organizational benefit to career coaching is that it allows you the opportunity to identify the performance deficiencies of your employees. You would normally do this through skills and interests inventories as well as observation and performance analysis. Once you identify the deficiencies, you can recommend develop strategies designed to overcome deficiencies. As a result, employees will be better trained and more productive.

As a career coach you can help your employees better understand the feelings they have about their careers. Such insights may help them make a greater commitment to their career and to the organization. Greater loyalty can improve the attitudes of all employees and can have a significant impact on the quality of the work they produce. Enhanced commitment can have a ripple effect for the organization that could help improve customer service, employee relations, and efficiency.

Career coaching also enables you to help your employees better understand their career choices. You can do this by providing them with information about their job and other opportunities within the organization. Before selecting a career path, most employees would like to know more about the job's advancement potential, requirements, activities and duties, and training requirements.

The organization benefits when employees believe that there are career opportunities for them. Turnover is one of the highest costs facing an organization. The recruiting, relocating, and training costs can cripple an organization and severely hurt its profitability. Therefore, it is in the best interests of the organization to keep its employees. Career coaching enables you to hold on to your most important asset, your people. For this reason alone career coaching is worth the effort.

Employees can gain greater insight into the organization through your efforts as a career coach. The more your employees know about the organization, the more loyal they will feel. Such insights can help your employees feel more a part of the organization rather than just one of its workers. This could improve teamwork and cooperation, and could help you build an ownership attitude among your employees.

Finally, career coaching allows employees to become more self-sufficient and independent. These very important qualities are critical in building self-directed and empowered work teams. Your efforts as a career coach could pay off nicely through improved quality, efficiency, and organizational performance.

## Why a Career Coach?

The primary purpose of career coaching is to help employees consider alternatives and make decisions regarding their careers. Another purpose is to provide organizations with information about their employees' career perspectives. Such information helps organizations to plan accordingly and to provide the opportunities necessary for employees to obtain their career objectives. To accomplish these purposes, as a career coach you must:

- Pose hypothetical questions to employees to expand their points of view regarding their careers.
- Uncover the underlying assumptions regarding an employee's career.
- Examine the seriousness of commitment that an employee has toward his or her career goals and objectives.
- Present different viewpoints to generate more in-depth analysis of career decisions and options.
- Analyze reasons for current career pursuits.
- Review career preferences.

## The Career Coaching Advantage

There are several advantages of becoming a career coach.[1] There are also some disadvantages, but they are outweighed by the positive results.

**Practical experience.**   Performance coaches have several years of experience on which to base their recommendations and

---

[1]J.W. Gilley and H.A. Moore, "Managers as Career Enhancers:  An Overlooked Resource," *Personnel Administrator* 31, no. 3, (1986), pp. 51–60.

suggestions. This may include working with more than one organization or in more than one area of responsibility in the same organization. Such experience can help the coach provide employees with greater insight into their career options.

Practical experience helps you to maintain a realistic approach to career counseling. It will enable you to share with employees real-life examples that help them to better understand the organization and make better career decisions. Finally, practical experience serves as a "developmental filter" for performance coaches. It can help you identify and prioritize training programs and developmental activities that helps improve employee performance. Ultimately, employees can benefit through advancement in their careers.

**Appraisals of opportunities.** While it is impossible to predict the future of any organization, experienced performance coaches are in an excellent position to know the opportunities available within their organization. This information can be used to guide and direct employees before they spend years preparing for jobs that are not in demand or not needed by the organization.

Performance coaches are more aware of the organizational climate and culture than are career counseling specialists. This is because they are involved daily with the people who determine the future direction of the organization and are integrated into the organization. Career counseling specialists are often viewed as outsiders by those within the organization. Because of this advantage, the performance coach can better identify the factors that impact the employees' career options and opportunities.

**Networking.** Like most people, you are most likely a member of several small groups that share a common purpose and identity. You communicate through informal channels, which together are known as the grapevine. The total of these groups and communication channels is referred to as your *network*.

Performance coaches who develop and maintain large networks can provide their employees greater access to information that is essential to their careers. In addition, networks enable their members to obtain information more quickly than through traditional communication channels. The weakness of a network is that the information may often be inaccurate.

**Better performance evaluations.** Many performance problems are career-related. Employees often feel trapped, stagnant, or overlooked. Many find little pleasure in their current job or occupation, which contributes to increased stress. If such negative feelings and stress continue, poor performance will also continue and may even become worse. Often, poorly performing employees either have lost their occupational mission in life or have been unable to identify their career purpose. Performance coaches can help employees regain their occupational mission or career purpose through career counseling activities. However, many performance coaches are reluctant to approach employees about performance problems. They often ignore the problem, hoping that somehow the situation will work itself out. However, ignoring performance problems further complicates them, and the manager is still held accountable for subordinates who are not performing up to their full potential or who fail to meet organizational expectations.

Performance evaluations provide an excellent opportunity to address career-related problems that affect performance. Performance coaches are in an ideal position to carry out such evaluations. You can use information from past performance evaluations to make realistic suggestions concerning career planning. Performance evaluations can also be used to identify deficiencies as well as strengths. You can use this information to recommend appropriate training activities designed to help improve employee performance. Such advice can greatly improve the organization's performance as well.

**Economic opportunities.** Many performance coaches are involved in strategic planning activities, which enable them to have a better understanding of the economic conditions that affect their organization. Furthermore, most performance coaches are responsible for managing financial resources such as budgets, making them more aware of economic conditions that have a positive and/or negative effect on specific careers and on their future.

**Similar career decisions.**   While the organizational landscape is ever changing, most career paths within an organization are similar. Thus, the decisions you have made regarding your career may be similar to those your employees face. As a performance coach, you have an opportunity to provide insight into the future by sharing the past. Such self-disclosures, while difficult, can provide confidence and assurance for your employees as they make career decisions. When you share your past career experiences, you are establishing the foundation for a better relationship with your employees.

Yet self-disclosure brings up two reasons why you might not want to become a career coach. First, employees have a right to privacy. Because it is sometimes difficult to determine when you are intruding, you may be reluctant to seek information about your employees' personal career decisions. In addition, you may be uncomfortable providing advice to employees regarding their career when you have not been asked to do so.

Second, you may face serious legal and ethical ramifications if you mishandle a career planning situation. For example, you could suggest to an employee a particular training program that could lead to a promotion. If the employee failed to be promoted after successfully completing the training program, you could be accused of incompetence and be blamed by the employee. The employee could seek retribution through legal action or tell other employees that he or she received poor advice from you. Either way, your reputation as a manager would be damaged. While situations like this one are quite rare, they could occur.

However, the advantages still outweigh the disadvantages, and we believe you can greatly influence the career planning and development of your employees. In order for you as a performance coach to be an effective problem solver and performance improver, you must become a skilled career coach. To accomplish this, you must (1) develop a better understanding of the career coaching process and (2) master interpersonal communication skills and techniques. We will examine the career coaching process next.

## THE CAREER COACHING PROCESS

Two important components of the career coaching process are the types of employees in an organization and the career selection process.

### The Three Types of Employees

Research shows that employees can be separated into three different groups. They are known as *movers, middle-of-the-road* employees, and *stuck* employees.[2] These three groups maintain different attitudes and behaviors toward their careers and organizations.

Movers view their careers as positive extensions of themselves. They live to work because work helps them define who they are as people. These employees are interested in learning new skills and finding new and exciting ways to apply what they have learned on the job. They approach work as a series of challenges, which helps them develop and prepare for the next opportunity. They have a long-term perspective on their career, and they assume that they will advance and grow. It could be said that movers are lifelong learners who see their career as a quest.

The middle-of-the-road employees provide balance in the workplace. Their career focus is stability. They want career challenges, but they are not going to jeopardize their current situation in order to acquire it. They view change as inherently bad. Job rotation is not perceived as a development opportunity but rather as a disruption in their daily routine.

The stuck employees have a negative perception of their careers. This leads to some adverse consequences, such as lack of vision, diminished self-esteem, disengagement from work, limited career orientation, and disruption and criticism toward the organization

---

[2]J.W. Gilley, "Career Development as a Partnership," *Personnel Administrator* 33, no. 4, (1988), pp. 62–68.

and fellow employees. Employees in this category fail to perform adequately and often leave the organization.

As a career coach, you must be able to identify and separate employees into their respective groups and address their career needs accordingly. You must provide the movers with ever-challenging assignments designed to develop their potential. When career advancement is not available, you should provide job enrichment opportunities to these employees. Whenever possible, you should allow movers to become involved in decisions regarding their career paths.

The biggest mistake managers make with middle-of-the-road employees is not believing their career is important to them. Because of this belief, you might make career recommendations that are inappropriate. One example would be not providing middle-of-the-road employees opportunities to learn and grow on the job. While advancement is not their principal motivator, making a solid contribution to the organization is of paramount importance. By limiting their growth and development opportunities, you would be preventing them from making such contributions.

Middle-of-the-road employees' careers are as important to them as movers' careers are to the movers. You have an excellent opportunity to provide middle-of-the-road employees with job enrichment experiences, because it allows them to grow and develop without the worry of advancement. You should also provide middle-of-the-road employees such opportunities in order to improve their performance and quality.

The stuck employees will provide you with your greatest challenge. The key to managing this type of employee is to discover what motivates him or her. They work to live, and their organizational commitment and loyalty are very low. What motivates stuck employees is often found outside of work. Their motivators may include such things as family, hobbies, sports, or recreational activities. Discovering the motivational factor and developing a strategy that enables the employee to obtain it through the job is essential. Perhaps simply talking about their interests with them will provide the spark they need to propel them to greater levels of accomplishment.

## Career Selection Process

As employees begin their careers, they are quick to discover, through a series of challenges, whether or not they have the skills and abilities to be successful. They also discover how well they like the work and whether their personal values match those of the organization. Over time, employees develop an occupational and career identity as well as a better understanding of their interests and needs.

Let's look at this process developmentally. It is commonly believed that career selection begins early in life. A person develops interests in certain types of tasks, activities, or subjects. These interests are then recognized through praise or rewards and lead to advanced development. Advanced development leads to abilities, which result in competencies. Again, achievement is rewarded, which motivates the person to work even harder toward proficiency. In the course of many years, the person develops an expertise that defines his or her career. In other words, the person will label himself or herself first as a consultant, manager, doctor, accountant, dentist, lawyer, salesperson, or other professional. Thus, *interests* leads to *abilities*, which lead to *competencies*, which lead to *proficiency*, which leads to *expertise*, which ultimately results in greater productivity for the person and higher profits for the organization.

As a career coach, you must help your employees incorporate the career selection process. To do this, you should ask each of your employees to outline his or her developmental process (see Figure 5.2). You should then discuss with each one how to improve that career path. Remember, the goal in career development is to develop career expertise that will benefit both the employee and the organization. Once you have discussed how to improve the personal career path, have each employee develop a plan for improvement to be submitted in writing on some future date. Identify a time to follow up with employees on the progress they are making. If possible, make completing this activity a part of the next performance review. This will increase the value of the experience.

# THE TECHNIQUES AND SKILLS OF EFFECTIVE CAREER COACHING

You may hesitate to offer career coaching to your employees because you lack formal training in psychology and counseling. The truth is, career coaching is less about psychology and counseling and more about good interpersonal communication skills. As a manager, you have had to rely on interpersonal communication skills for years. Therefore, you have developed at least some of the skills you need to become a career coach.

Because interpersonal communications are essential to you as a manager, we could assume you have developed superior skills in this area. However, most of us have never been formally trained in interpersonal communications—most of what you know has been acquired through trial and error. Even fewer managers have been taught how to use interpersonal communication skills in career coaching. Let's take a look at the interpersonal skills and techniques required to ensure that career coaching is successful.

Our attention will be focused on three areas: (1) using participatory communications, (2) developing a positive communications climate, and (3) using interpersonal communication skills.[3]

## *Technique 1: Participatory Communications*

Using participatory communications will require you to shift your managerial style from authoritarian to participatory. You must relinquish control and dominance over employees and allow them to participate as equal partners in examining their careers. The participatory approach will also require you to develop a positive working relationship with employees. The creation of this type of relationship begins when you recognize that employees bring a

---

[3]J.W. Gilley and S.A. Eggland, *Principles of Human Resource Development* (Reading, MA: Addison-Wesley, 1989), pp. 59–62.

great deal of experience to the organization—an invaluable asset to be acknowledged, tapped, and used.

The participatory approach is relatively nonthreatening to employees and requires their active participation in the career coaching process. Participation helps employees support the decisions they have to make regarding their careers.

### Technique 2: The Positive Communications Climate

You can use the participatory approach only when you encourage a free exchange of ideas, opinions, and feelings. Employees benefit from a positive communications climate because they feel more secure and can speak freely about issues affecting their careers. Such a climate is considered comfortable, conducive to sharing, and even nurturing for employee development. A sharing climate goes beyond the superficial to demonstrate a deep concern for the well-being of employees and is dedicated to the improvement of interpersonal relations.

### Technique 3: Interpersonal Communication Skills

Once you have established a positive communications climate, you can use several interpersonal communication skills to produce positive outcomes during career coaching. These skills can help you gather information from your employees, help you understand them, help them communicate their point of view, encourage them to share their feelings, and provide a moment of silence so that your employees can gather their thoughts. These skills serve as a guide in the career coaching process.

Learning to be an effective career coach is a difficult task for many managers. Our approach simplifies the learning process by focusing on single skill cluster so you can concentrate on a set of skills rather than on a single skill. This will enable you to learn more efficiently. You can concentrate on mastering one skill cluster at a time, see yourself readily improve in that area, and then move to another cluster. When all of the skill clusters are mastered, you can integrate them and use them to become a more effective career coach.

The interpersonal communication skill clusters and related specific skills are as follows:[4]

| Skill Cluster | Specific Skill |
| --- | --- |
| Attending skills | Acceptance |
| | Attentiveness |
| | Nonverbal techniques |
| | Empathy |
| | Being genuine |
| | Rapport |
| | Understanding |
| Following skills | Active listening |
| | Encouraging |
| | Questioning |
| | Silence |
| Reflecting skills | Paraphrasing |
| | Clarifying |
| | Interpreting |
| | Summarizing |

**Attending skills.** Attending skills are the common nonverbal communication and relationship-building skills you should use in paying careful attention to your employees when they speak. They help you build the proper communications climate. Attending skills include acceptance, attentiveness, nonverbal techniques, empathy, genuineness, rapport, and understanding.[5] Each of these seven ingredients helps ensure that a positive, comfortable, and nonthreatening communications climate exists between you and your employees—one that encourages your employees to discuss career alternatives and options openly and without fear of

---

[4]R. Bolton, *People Skills: How to Assert Yourself, Listen to Others, and Resolve Conflict* (New York: Simon & Schuster, 1986), p. 33.

[5]J.W. Gilley and S.A. Eggland, *Marketing HRD within Organizations: Enhancing the Visibility, Effectiveness, and Credibility of Programs* (San Francisco: Jossey-Bass, 1992), pp. 176–77.

reprisals. As you create an environment of trust, the relationship you have with your employees will be strengthened.

*Acceptance.*   We define acceptance as a warm regard for people as individuals of unconditional self-worth, no matter how negative or positive their behavior might be. Acceptance is the basic attitude that requires you to respect your employees as persons of worth. Because each employee is a complex person made up of differing experiences, values, and attitudes, it is essential that you value differences. You can demonstrate acceptance by allowing employees to differ from one another.

*Attentiveness.*   Attentiveness refers to your efforts to hear the messages communicated by employees. It requires skill in active listening, which is described below. Interrupting your employee so you can present your point of view diminishes the importance of the employee's ideas and communicates a lack of respect for him or her. On the other hand, listening sends the message that you are interested in, and sensitive to, your employee's feelings and thoughts.

*Nonverbal techniques.*   Nonverbal techniques are also important in establishing and maintaining a positive communications climate. Many employees are quite aware of the nonverbal behavior of managers and may often avoid you as a result. Simple techniques such as maintaining proper eye contact can greatly improve your effectiveness as a career coach.

*Empathy.*   Typically, empathy has been described as putting yourself in the other person's shoes—in other words, attempting to see things from another person's vantage point. Empathic understanding is the ability to recognize, sense, and understand the feelings of another person. It is also the ability to accurately communicate this understanding to that person. It is not enough for you to understand the behaviors or feelings of employees; you must also communicate that understanding to them.

Performance coaches who have the ability to relate to the feelings of their employees can be considered empathic.

*Being genuine.*   Being genuine refers to your ability to be yourself in all situations rather than playing a part or role. Genuineness is demonstrated when you know your true feelings and communicate them when necessary. Being genuine implies honesty and candor with yourself while functioning as a career coach. You should not pretend to be something you're not. Being genuine also implies self-disclosure, but does not mean a total unveiling of your personal and private life. Employees want to believe in you; honesty and candor provide the proper atmosphere for this to take place.

*Rapport.*   Rapport may be defined as an unconditional positive relationship between you and your employees. Rapport is more than a superficial relationship; it is a deep concern for the well-being of your employees. Rapport is established through your sincere interest in, and acceptance of, your employees. The result of developing rapport is the creation of a positive working relationship. It can be observed when you are equally concerned for the relationship you have with your employees and the tasks they complete.

*Understanding.*   Acknowledging that you will never fully understand your employees, it can be said that *trying* to understand them is one of the essential ingredients in the career coaching process. In other words, as employees express themselves in verbal and nonverbal ways, you must attempt to understand them.

Understanding can be characterized as external or internal. External understanding refers to your ability to understand the behaviors of your employees. This means being able to identify employees' behaviors and to react accordingly. Internal understanding refers to your ability to step into the perceptual world of your employees in an effort to discover their fears, concerns, and anxieties. This type of understanding is necessary for real communication to take place.

**Following skills.**   One of your primary tasks as a career coach will be to stay out of your employees' way so you can discover how they view their situation. Unfortunately, the average manager interrupts and diverts his or her employees by asking too many questions or making too many statements. It is common for managers to talk so much during career coaching that they monopolize the conversation. As a result, they don't have a clue what their employees are thinking or feeling.

We believe that there are four following skills that foster communications: active listening, encouraging, questioning, and silence.[6]

*Active listening.*   During career coaching, you can gather information from your employees through verbal and nonverbal cues. Using these cues, you can concentrate on what your employees are saying about their careers. This process, known as active listening, will help you become more involved during the conversation.

When you actively listen to your employees, you can better understand their intended meaning. You also convey respect to them as people. Active listening can produce several positive results, namely, attentively listened-to employees will tend to:

- Consider their point of view as important.
- State their feelings and thoughts clearly.
- Listen to other employees carefully when they speak.
- Become less confrontational than before.
- Become receptive to differing points of view.

Active listening is an important bridge to understanding employees because it changes your entire relationship. Not only is active listening essential in career coaching, but as much as 80 percent of your time is spent in communicating, and over half of that time involves listening. Feedback is also a necessary ingredient of

---

[6]Ibid., pp. 180–84.

effective communication, and feedback can become helpful only through good listening.

We have identified the following desirable listening behaviors to help you develop good listening skills:

1. Concentrating all your physical and mental energies on listening.
2. Avoiding interrupting your employees.
3. Demonstrating interest and alertness.
4. Seeking areas of agreement with the employee.
5. Searching for meanings and not getting hung up on specific words.
6. Demonstrating patience; remember, you can listen faster than the employee can speak.
7. Providing clear and unambiguous feedback to the employee.
8. Repressing the tendency to respond emotionally to what is said.
9. Asking questions when you do not understand something.
10. Withholding evaluation of the message until the employee is finished and you are sure you understand the message.

*Encouraging.*   This technique enables employees to elaborate about their feelings and thoughts. Using supportive remarks such as "I understand," "It's OK to feel that way," "That is interesting, tell me more," or "I hear you" are useful in countering feelings of inadequacy on the part of the employee. They encourage the employee to continue the discussion. Another effective technique is to use a nod of the head and an "Mm-hm." They can serve to strengthen the employee response and his or her efforts to continuing speaking. This technique lets the employee know the manager is listening, without interrupting.

*Questioning.*   Questioning is a common but often overused career coaching technique. You should use questions only to obtain specific information or to direct the conversation to be more constructive and informative.

While questions are often overused, they remain powerful tools that can facilitate discussion, guide the flow and direction of conversation, and help you obtain specific information very quickly. Basically, there are two types of questions used in career coaching: open ended and closed ended. Open-ended questions generally require more than a few words to answer and allow employees to expand their thoughts. They also help employees explain their points of view thoroughly. Open-ended questions allow employees to respond differently to the same question, for example: "Could you tell me how you feel about the quality of your work during the last quarter?" Several different responses could be given in answering this type of question. While you may be looking for a specific response, an open-ended question is less threatening to employees and allows them to convey their points of view.

In contrast, closed-ended questions are ones that can be answered in relatively few words and have specific responses. They are important for gathering essential information, that is, for obtaining the facts you need during a discussion between you and your employees. This type of question also minimizes personal interaction. An example of a closed-ended question might be "Bill, how long have you been an Accountant II?" or "Mary, do you think it will take more than two years for you to develop the skills you need to be promoted to property manager?" When you use closed-ended questions you are not concerned with the feelings of your employees but rather in gathering needed information.

*Silence.* Although a somewhat difficult technique to master, the use of silence enables employees to think through what has transpired during a conversation. It also allows them to share additional information or explanations if appropriate or needed.

You may be uncomfortable with silence as a technique when you first use it. But the use of intentional silence provides employees additional time to think about what they are going to say and allows them to explore feelings more deeply. These benefits should help encourage you to overcome your reluctance to use this technique.

Silence may provide less articulate employees the opportunity to explain their thoughts or feelings more thoroughly. This may help them gain self-confidence and may improve their self-worth.

While the benefits of silence are many, silence can be overdone; more than a minute of silence, for example, may cause discomfort for you and your employees. Therefore, you will want to avoid extensive periods of silence, which may be misinterpreted and perceived as unresponsiveness. Silence is most useful when used in combination with other techniques such as encouraging and active listening.

**Reflective skills.**   Good career coaches respond reflectively to what employees are saying. They restate, in their own words, the feeling and/or content that is being expressed. There are four basic reflecting skills.[7] In paraphrasing you focus on the employee's content. The reflection of feelings occurs when you concentrate on feeling words, and infer feelings from general comments. You use clarifying and interpreting skills to identify feelings. The combined reflection of feelings and content is called the reflection of meaning. Summarizing skills are used to recap the most significant elements of a long conversation.

*Paraphrasing.*   Paraphrasing is when a listener attempts to restate, in his or her own words, the speaker's basic message. As a performance coach, your primary purpose in paraphrasing will be to test your understanding of what has been said. Another purpose of paraphrasing is to communicate to the employee that you are trying to understand the employee's basic message. If the paraphrasing is successful, it demonstrates that you have been following the employee during his or her verbal explorations. An example of paraphrasing would be "You seem to be saying that your supervisor's overbearing nature makes it difficult for you to do a good job."

---

[7]Ibid., pp. 185–86.

*Clarifying.*   You can make clarifying statements in order to better understand employees' feelings and attitudes. You can also ask employees to elaborate on a particular point to clarify the meaning. It may be helpful to ask employees to give an example to better illustrate their point of view. Remember, this technique should not be used to interpret feelings or to identify the cause of a problem. This technique should only be used to clarify your understanding. An example of this technique would be "Are you upset for not being selected to participate in a team-building workshop?"

*Interpreting.*   When using the technique of interpreting, you go beyond the employee's statements to explain cause-and-effect relationships and to clarify implications. This technique enables the employee to understand more fully all of the ramifications of what he or she is saying. Using this technique generally results in a greater awareness of the motives and causes of career problems. You can also draw a conclusion regarding the employee's perspective of his or her career using this technique. The problem with this technique is that your interpretation is subject to error.

As a technique, interpretation provides a basis for publicly testing any assumptions made by your employees. Thus, it allows employees the opportunity to acknowledge the correctness of your interpretations as well as to verify their own point of view. Some of the most common interpretation statements include "What I hear you saying . . ." and "Based on what you have said . . ."

*Summarizing.*   You use this technique to identify the key points of ideas discussed during the conversation. You may ask the employee to agree or disagree with the summary in order to make certain that both sides understand each other. An example of a summarizing statement would be "Let me take a moment to summarize our conversation."

Summarizing differs from paraphrasing in that it is used at the end of the discussion with your employees. A summarizing technique deals with several thoughts and ideas. It also helps you determine the most appropriate steps to follow. Sometimes, you may want to ask your employees to summarize the discussion. This is another way to check for accuracy and understanding.

## BECOMING SKILLED AS A CAREER COACH

As a career coach, you can help your employees make better career decisions, and help the organization better allocate their human resources. You can help employees gain greater insights into the organization, enhance their self-sufficiency, and help them better understand their feelings regarding their careers. Career coaching can help the organization reduce recruiting and hiring costs, improve performance, enhance teamwork, and improve quality and profitability.

## Chapter Eight

# The Manager as Confronter

## *The Performance Coaching Process*

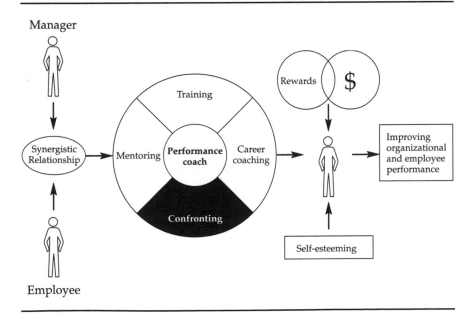

One of the most important performance coaching roles to the organization is that of confronter. It is during this role that your entire attention is focused on improving performance and resolving problems. The greatest benefits to the organization can be realized through your execution of this role.

The organization can benefit through improving quality and performance, which will enhance organizational efficiency and effectiveness. Such improvements can help the organization to become more competitive in the marketplace. This can increase market share and lead to higher profits. As a confronter, you will be responsible for identifying performance shortfalls of your employees. In order to accomplish this, you must identify performance standards. Once these are identified, you must communicate them to all your employees so that they can use them to focus their performance. Performance standards can be used to help you create critical performance measures, which are designed to compare actual performance with desired performance. When performance falls short of the standards, you must determine why your employees are failing to perform adequately.

There are many possible reasons for the lack of performance. First, your employees may not know *what* to do. In other words, the job responsibilities or job description has not been fully communicated to them. Therefore, employees either fail to perform the behaviors in the correct sequence or drop certain critical behaviors. Second, employees may not know *how* to do their jobs. This is often because of skill deficiencies. Skill deficiencies are generally overcome through training activities. You should identify the appropriate performance strategy and provide the necessary training. Third, there may be *barriers* or *conflicts* in the work environment or among co-workers that either prevent or discourage the adequate performance of tasks and responsibilities. Your responsibility is to identify, prevent, and/or resolve such barriers or conflicts. Finally, employees may not do what you desire because they simply don't *want* to. This is a serious problem that you must solve before your employees can perform to the required standards.

However, even after they know the reasons many managers have difficulty confronting employees who don't perform adequately. They will often avoid the situation, hoping that it will somehow work itself out. They hope and pray that employees will improve without having to confront them. When such managers do finally get around to confronting their employees, they tend to overdo it by making the confrontation personal rather than focusing on the performance problem. As a result, emotions explode, things are said, feelings are hurt, and everyone resents everyone else. Furthermore, performance doesn't get any better. The outcomes are poorer employee relationships and a "never again" attitude on the part of the manager.

Regardless, it is still your job to make certain that your employees meet or exceed the performance standards. We believe that focusing your attention on resolving conflicts (problem 3) and solving motivation problems (problem 4) will enable you to improve your employees' performance while maintaining a positive relationship. In the next few pages, we will provide you with the necessary tools to become an excellent performance confronter.

## THE CONFRONTER ROLE

In order for your employees to enhance their professional growth, make a commitment to continual performance improvement, and accept increasingly difficult tasks and responsibilities, you must master the art of confronting. To accomplish this, you can rely on three critical sets of skills. Each will help you improve the interpersonal relationships between you and your employees, as well as improve their performance.

The three sets of skills are as follows:

1. *Assertion skills:* Using verbal and nonverbal assertion skills will enable you to maintain respect, satisfy your needs, and defend your rights without manipulating, dominating, or controlling your employees.

2. *Conflict-resolution skills:* These skills will enable you to deal with the emotional turbulence that typically accompanies conflicts.

3. *Collaborative problem-solving skills:* These skills include ways of resolving conflicts and problems that will satisfy you, your employees, and the organization.

 Before discussing each set of skills in more detail, let's look at some ways you may have been "killing performance."


## THE 12 PERFORMANCE KILLERS

Sometimes the most well-intentioned and innocent comments can backfire. They can prevent your employees from trying new skills, resolving conflicts, and solving problems. They can damage communications and hurt your employees' confidence. They can also reduce employees' self-esteem. We call them the 12 performance killers because they can negatively impact or shut down employee performance if used at the wrong time or in the wrong way. We cluster them into three categories: judging, providing solutions, and avoiding.[1]

 **Judging.**   Four of the performance killers fall into this category—criticizing, diagnosing, labeling, and praising. They are all variations on a common theme, which is judging your employees. Judging places you in a superior position, which makes it difficult for you to build and maintain a positive relationship with your employees.

 *Criticizing.*   Making negative comments about your employees' performance, attitudes, and decisions is a form of criticism. For many managers criticism is a way of life—a negative way.

---

[1]T. Gordon, *Parent Effectiveness Training: The "No-Loss" Program for Raising Responsible Children* (New York: Peter H. Wyden, 1970), pp. 44, 108.

*Diagnosing.* Playing amateur psychiatrist is a common way some managers relate to their employees. Comments like "I can read them like a book" get in the way of meaningful communication. Presenting employees with an analysis of why they are behaving in a certain way doesn't really help improve their performance. It just forces them to defend their behavior.

*Labeling.* Some managers stereotype their employees by placing them into categories. Most labeling has either negative overtones or a stigma attached. Such comments as "All you college boys are alike," or "Women are too emotional to be managers" put employees into boxes that can't possibly describe all their good qualities and attributes.

*Praising.* Praising your employees can be a two-edged sword. Praising calls for an evaluation of your employees, which requires you to place yourself in a superior position. It can be seen as manipulative and disingenuous. Employees may wonder why you're praising them and may then be waiting for the other shoe to fall. Praising employees too much or without real cause can hurt your relationship in the long run.

**Providing solutions.** Another set of performance killers is related to providing solutions for your employees. You might be asking yourself, I thought I got paid to solve problems? You do, but the way you communicate solutions can be perceived negatively. Your behaviors may be seen as aggressive, authoritative, and demeaning. Providing a solution often compounds a problem or creates a new problem without resolving the original dilemma. This set includes advising, ordering, moralizing, questioning, and threatening.

*Advising.* Giving your employees "the solution" to their problem in a way that interferes with their ability to solve it for themselves is a case of negative advising. It's what we call "If I were you . . ." statements. Such statements severely restrict employees' growth and development, and force them to be totally dependent on you.

*Ordering.*   Ordering is simply a solution sent coercively and backed up by force. It is a process of commanding your employees to do what you want to have done. This approach may cause some employees to become resentful, and it may cause them to sabotage the results. Other employees who are constantly being ordered around become very compliant and submissive.

*Moralizing.*   When you use this performance killer you are telling your employees what they "should do" rather than helping them decide the best solution. Moralizing is demoralizing. It fosters resentment and anxiety.

*Questioning.*   We refer to this as the "Sergeant Friday routine." Everything is questioned. Your employees have to defend every single decision and action. Their judgment is always suspect, and their decisions are never good enough.

*Threatening.*   In threatening, you are trying to control your employees' actions by warning of negative consequences that you instigate. "You'll do it or else . . . " is the attitude that prevails. Because no one wants to be threatened, the threats will produce immediate defensive behavior. Threatening rarely works.

**Avoiding.**   Managers use several techniques that cause conversations and performance to get off track. Limit emotional involvement with employees when addressing performance problems and conflicts. These techniques include diverting, logical argument, and reassuring.

*Diverting.*   One of the most common ways managers switch conversations with their employees is called diverting. It's a form of mental distraction. It enables you to change topics and avoid addressing the ones of interest to your employees. Diverting is also used to avoid an uncomfortable conversation with employees. It sometimes occurs because of a lack of effective listening skills. Regardless of the reason, diverting causes employees to feel that their concerns, feelings, and opinions are not very important.

*Logical argument.*   Some managers have difficulty dealing with their employees' feelings and emotions, so they use logic to avoid addressing them. Logic is very important, but it has its place. Most interpersonal conflicts are emotion laden and the manager must confront them accordingly. When you use logic to avoid emotional involvement, you are withdrawing from your employees at a most inopportune moment.

*Reassuring.*   Many managers try to stop their employees from feeling the negative emotions they are experiencing. They say things like "Don't worry about it" or "It will all work out OK in the end." They think they're comforting their employees while they're actually doing the opposite. Reassurance is a form of emotional withdrawal because you can offer it without really getting involved.

## USING ASSERTION SKILLS TO IMPROVE PERFORMANCE

When you confront your employees regarding their performance, you can demonstrate one of three types of behavior. Each has a different effect on your employees. The behaviors include aggressive, submissive, and assertive.

### Aggressive Behavior

Aggressive managers express their feelings, needs, and ideas at the expense of their employees. They almost always win arguments. Aggressive managers get things done but are often abusive, rude, and sarcastic. They may berate employees for poor performance, dominate them, and insist on having the final word on topics of conversation important to them. Aggressive managers tend to overpower their employees. Their point of view is "This is what I want done; what you want is of little importance or no importance at all." Such an attitude can force some employees into better performance, but most employees will find ways to subvert and undermine such a manager.

## Submissive Behavior

Some managers have difficulty confronting their employees. They are the opposite of the aggressive manager. Most submissive managers let their employees dictate the level and quality of their performance. Most submissive managers do not express their honest feelings, needs, values, and concerns. They allow their employees to violate them by denying them their rights, and ignoring their requests. Submissive managers rarely state their desires and expectations directly. Some do, but in such an apologetic and diffident manner that they often are not taken seriously. Sometimes they think they have spoken clearly, but their messages are coded to such an extent that their employees don't understand what they mean. Nonverbal behavior like a shrug of the shoulder, lack of eye contact, an excessively soft voice, or hesitating speech may undercut their expression of desire or expectation.

## Assertive Behavior

Assertive managers use methods of communication that enable them to maintain self-respect, personal happiness, and satisfaction. They defend their right to manage employees without abusing or dominating them. Assertive managers stand up for their own rights and express their personal needs, values, concerns, and ideas in direct and appropriate ways. While meeting their own needs, they don't violate the needs of their employees. True assertiveness is a way of behaving that confirms the manager's own individual worth and dignity while simultaneously confirming and maintaining the worth and dignity of the employees.

After comparing them with assertive behaviors, you can see that aggressive and submissive behaviors can create additional conflicts. Aggressive managers may get a lot of work done, but their employees resent and dislike them. Aggressive managers produce a work environment full of tension and hostility. Submissive managers may be liked by their employees but not respected. The submissive manager's work environment is one of chaos and confusion; conflict between employees is common because there is no one to mediate and control negative interactions.

To become a competent confronter, you must balance your need to get the work done with your need to be a friend to your employees. You can achieve this balance by being assertive. You will have a more fulfilling relationship with your employees and improve productivity by communicating your needs, expectations, and concerns in a way that demonstrates respect for your employees. An assertive message contains three parts:

1. A nonjudgmental description of the performance behaviors to be changed.
2. A disclosure of your feelings.
3. A clarification of the effects of the employee's behavior on you.[2]

**Nonjudgmental description of behavior.** Your description should be specific so that your employees know precisely what you mean. Otherwise, they may not clearly understand what behavior you find unacceptable. You should avoid drawing inferences about their motives or attitudes but focus on their behavior: "what they did" that concerns you. Your behavioral descriptions should be as brief as possible in order to avoid confusion. Try to make your descriptions an objective statement rather than a judgment. In other words, don't imply that, because their performance is not adequate in one area, your employees are lazy, stupid, or bad.

---

[2]R. Bolton, *People Skills: How to Assert Yourself, Listen to Others, and Resolve Conflict* (New York: Simon & Schuster, 1986), p. 140.

The following are some examples of nonjudgmental behavioral descriptions:

- When you are frequently late for work . . .
- When you overspend your budget . . .
- When you don't take accurate phone messages . . .
- When you don't turn in your report on time . . .

We will use these examples later to illustrate the other two parts of an assertive message.

**Disclosure of feelings.** The second part of an assertive message allows managers to communicate how they feel about their employees' behavior. It is a genuine disclosure of the emotions you are experiencing as a result of your employees' behavior. The easiest way of expressing how you feel when an employee's performance is unacceptable is to use "I" messages. In other words, "I feel . . ." describes what is going on inside. You can identify the feelings immediately after an inadequate or poor performance.

**Clarification of the effects of the behavior.** What we mean by *effects* are those things that directly impact you as a result of your employees' behavior. For example, money, time, extra work, quality, and teamwork are all things affected by your employees' behavior.

Let's look again at the four previous examples of nonjudgmental behavior descriptions, and add a disclosure of feelings and clarification of effects for each:

- When you are frequently late for work . . . I feel angry . . . because it costs us money to delay the production line.
- When you overspend your budget . . . I feel annoyed . . . because it means I must make cuts that will affect the quality of the project.
- When you don't take accurate telephone messages . . . I feel upset . . . because I lack information and can't return calls that may be important.

- When you don't turn in your report on time . . . I feel frustrated . . . because I can't get an accurate picture of our current financial position.

Your use of assertive messages can greatly enhance your employees' understanding of your concerns and feelings, and the effects of their behavior. These messages should help you and your employees to remain rational in difficult times.

## MASTERING AND RESOLVING CONFLICT

Most managers would like to live their lives without conflict, but to be human is to experience conflict. Some conflict is positive, while other conflict is negative. You forget about the conflicts that improve quality and performance because they're not viewed as conflict. They're perceived as troubleshooting or problem-solving efforts. But make no mistake about it, they are conflicts because there is a difference between what you *have* and what you *want*. Negative conflicts are a different story. They are remembered forever. In fact, managerial war stories are almost always about some overwhelming conflict that a manager was able to conquer.

### *Negative Reactions to Conflict*

Many managers and employees react to conflict inappropriately. There are five fairly common reactions to conflict: acquiescing, avoiding, defensiveness, denying, and dominating.[3] While each may appear to have short-term benefits, used repeatedly it can lead to serious negative consequences.

**Acquiescing.** Many employees acquiesce when confronted by conflict. They give in, often without a struggle. The biggest mistake you can make is to think your employees agree with you or your solution just because they are willing to go along. Even if they do disagree with you, they may not say anything because

---

[3]Ibid., pp. 234–236.

they don't want to deal with the conflict. As a result, they go through their organizational life without getting their needs met.

When employees habitually acquiesce, they may harbor deep resentment toward you without your being aware of it. They may even sabotage projects, proposals, and/or teamwork because they feel dominated and abused. You might expect them to speak up for themselves and voice their concerns, but that might lead to a conflict they don't want to deal with.

**Avoiding.**   Beyond those who acquiesce, some managers and employees are even less tolerant of conflict; they simply do everything possible to avoid dealing with it. Some employees change the subject to avoid conflict, while others gloss over the problem, acting as though it doesn't exist. Some use silence as a way to avoid addressing the real issues that cause conflicts.

Some managers believe conflicts can injure and harm their employee relationships, so they use avoidance as a method of maintaining a healthy relationship with their employees. This creates a paradox because avoiding conflicts undermines this relationship and can produce isolation and denial.

**Defensiveness.**   Several years ago, we heard an employee describe the conflict she had with her managers as a "surprise attack." Because she was not prepared for the conflict, she could only react to it—and react she did. Some employees feel attacked during a conflict and react by counterattacking. Before long, the little conflict has turned into an all-out war. This is what we call the upward spiral of conflict.

It is a natural tendency of humans to be defensive. You push back when you feel you're being pushed. We will address this condition in more detail and discuss strategies designed to overcome this type of reaction when we examine assertiveness skills later in this chapter.

**Denying.**   Conflicts are sometimes so threatening that managers and employees deny their existence. They rationalize their behavior and try to ignore the conflict. In other words, they pretend to themselves and to others that everything is all right and that they are not affected by the conflict. The reality is just the opposite: Things couldn't be worse. In such cases, managers need to deal with the causes of the conflict.

**Dominating.** Dominating occurs when a manager imposes a solution to a conflict on his or her employees. The solution is one that meets the manager's needs, not necessarily those of the employees. In fact, it may not even be the best solution to the conflict.

Dominating is the most aggressive type of reaction to a conflict. It is common for the dominating person to verbally attack anyone who disagrees with his or her proposed solution. This is done to control the people involved and to ensure the outcome.

Such an authoritarian approach to resolving conflicts can be very damaging to the relationship you have with your employees. Dominating tends to break the will of your employees, and it severely limits their spontaneity and independence. While it may be effective in resolving a conflict, it puts employees down and it can cripple any future attempts you would make to encourage empowerment or self-direction.

## Benefits of Conflict

We believe that you and your employees can benefit from conflict because it provides you an opportunity to express your thoughts and feelings openly. Conflict allows you to share your perspective and express your passion. It gives you and your employees an excuse to come together and function as a team.

We believe that without conflict you cannot find the personal intimacy needed to build strong, self-esteeming relationships. Conflict is the fire that hardens a relationship to be able to withstand the everyday trials and tribulations of corporate life. Conflict helps prevent stagnation and complacency among you and your employees. It stimulates interest and curiosity, and fosters creativity. Conflict can even force you out of your sheeplike passivity to invent new and exciting solutions to difficult situations. For example, most performance and technological improvements occur because of a conflict. As a catalyst for change, conflict causes you to address the status quo and to find better methods of production and service.

Conflict is a necessary ingredient of organizational renewal. It can provide an organization the motivation and energies necessary to take action. It forces organizational leaders to function at their highest levels of innovativeness, and it allows for the greatest diversity of viewpoints to be expressed among employees. Finally, conflict forces managers to articulate their views and to bring forth the arguments needed to help foster changes required within the organization.

## Organizational Conditions that Create Conflict

The way an organization is structured has an effect on the amounts and types of conflict created. For example, bureaucratic organizations, which are hierarchical, have many layers of management and several competing units and divisions. These layers serve as natural barriers to communication and teamwork, which can produce mistrust and foster inefficiency. Both can create serious conflicts for you and your employees.

Competitive organizations, which promote a sink-or-swim attitude among their employees, consist of many talented and skilled people. However, only a few are loyal to the organization and most will leave if their needs are not met. Threats like this may place extreme pressure on you to maintain a balance between the needs of the organization and the needs of its employees.

Many passive organizations believe that their human resources are easy to replace, which makes it difficult for you to encourage training activities designed to improve performance—a real conflict if you believe in developing your employees.

Your personality and leadership style are also sources of conflict. For example, you may be a collaborative and supportive manager who encourages your employees to be independent and

self-directed. However, one of your supervisors may be very autocratic and domineering. The supervisor wants to control the employees and make all the decisions. These two styles clash, which
can be a major source of conflict.

Let's further complicate this situation. The employees within
your unit are split right down the middle. Half of them prefer your
style and approach, while the other half prefer your supervisor's
style and approach. Conflict caused by differing leadership styles
can divide teams, departments, units, and entire organizations—
and can lead to devastating results.

Organizational working environments can also cause conflict.
Some employees prefer a win–lose environment, while others
want a team-oriented one. Some employees want to be told what
to do every minute of the day, while others want independence
and freedom in their work environment. The amount and degree
of change desired in an organization can also create conflict. Some
employees are very comfortable with change, while others are not.
The methods you use to communicate change can be a source of
tension for some employees. Some prefer to be told in person,
while others prefer a small-group or team approach. Some employees want to know exactly what the outcomes of change will
be, while others could not care less.

Conflict is not just between people. It can be present in the very
fabric of the organization, and if so you must confront it in order to
improve employee performance and solve problems.

### Types of Conflict

Not all conflicts are the same. There are three basic types of conflict.[4] The most common type is conflict of emotions, which occurs
because people are human and differences are inevitable. You and
your employees will have strong feelings that sometimes can become antagonistic. Conflict of emotions can be addressed and

---

[4]Ibid., p. 233.

overcome using a **four-step conflict resolution process,** described in the next section of this chapter.

The second type of conflict is known as conflict of need. Within the organization, substantive issues must be resolved by managers and employees. You often refer to this activity as problem solving. But at the root of any problem-solving efforts are needs that are in conflict. Therefore, you should use a collaborative problem-solving approach in order to address and satisfy all the needs present. We will provide a **seven-step collaborative problem-solving** method later in this chapter.

Conflict of values is the third type. There is rarely any acceptable solution to this type of conflict because nothing concrete is involved. Values are deeply embedded in our minds, and our behavior is directly influenced by them. They are not easily changed or compromised. You can apply the conflict resolution techniques described below to help you better understand, appreciate, and build tolerance for your employees' values; however, you will not be able to eliminate serious value differences. You must learn to live with them, or part company.

These three types of conflict are referred to as *realistic conflict* because you can address, manage, and resolve them. However, there are some conflicts you cannot resolve. They stem from prejudice; ignorance; dysfunctional organizational teams, groups, and structures; and win–lose environments. We refer to these types of conflicts as *nonrealistic*. These conflicts can only be addressed, managed, and resolved by senior executives and managers because they require top-level and organization-wide attention.

## CONFLICT RESOLUTION METHOD

The conflict resolution method should be thought of as a set of skills that help you govern conflict. It can also be seen as a constructive process for handling emotion-laden disagreements between you and your employees. This process encourages assertive communication and the sharing of feelings, but it does not permit the typical verbal free-for-all, which blocks creative resolution of conflict and tends to be very destructive of relationships. The four steps of the methods are (1) acknowledging conflict, (2) clarifying the conflict, (3) problem solving, and (4) confirming the answer.

When conflict occurs, you should not become defensive. Most conflicts are simply the result of different perspectives. Imagine two people looking at different sides of a dollar bill. One is convinced he is seeing everything; the details and images are clear. The other one, who is looking at the other side of the same dollar bill, sees things quite differently. She too is convinced that she is seeing the entire dollar bill. But she is seeing things he can't see, and before too long each is trying to tell the other what the dollar *really* looks like. The truth is that they're both right but their realities—or points of view— are different: conflict pure and simple.

### *Acknowledging Conflict*

The conflict resolution method begins with acknowledging conflict.[5] This is very critical because both parties must be willing to agree that arguing and fighting over differences of opinion will accomplish very little. In addition, acknowledging that a conflict exists helps with controlling the emotions and feelings associated with differences of opinion.

This step consists of two activities: listening and sharing. Let's look at them in more detail. Listening carefully to what your employees are saying is the first step in resolving conflict. Usually, but not always, employees' words are an accurate reflection of what they are thinking. Most negative statements made by employees are a way of verbalizing excess tension or fear. The very process of converting tension into words serves to reduce the tension, even if the words themselves don't actually reveal its nature or the reason for it.

---

[5]J.W. Gilley and S.A. Eggland, *Marketing HRD within Organizations: Enhancing Visibility, Effectiveness, and Credibility of Programs* (San Francisco: Jossey-Bass, 1992), p. 194.

Negative statements deflate themselves through the process of tension being converted into words, if they are allowed to flow uninterrupted. So the first, best, and easiest way to deflate negative statements is to listen to them, without interruption and with sincere interest.

What happens if you don't listen? Too often, you may take the employees' negative statements as a personal attack. Instead of analyzing and diagnosing what they are saying, you may allow the statements to produce tension. However, you can learn to manage this tension successfully through the mutual process of sharing.

Sharing is a form of support. Positive interpersonal relations are based on your ability to share feelings with someone. Thus, when you use statements like "I understand how you feel," or "I guess I'm not surprised to find you feeling that way," or "You seem to feel strongly about that," you are reflecting and sharing someone's feelings. Real interpersonal relations are built not on a technique or skill, but on a caring attitude. You help your employees reduce tension by showing them that you understand how they feel and that you are not surprised or upset. When your employees sense your confidence and calm behavior, it bolsters theirs. Show your employees that you understand how they feel, and do or say nothing that might increase their tension or fear.

### Clarifying Conflict

The second step is to clarify your employees' thinking so that they are willing to receive new and logical information.[6] If there is one thing known to human nature, it is that no one likes to look bad. So when your employees make a negative statement, you have to make it easy for them to withdraw gracefully.

Few employees are ready and willing to reveal the true motives behind their behavior, even when they understand what these are. They learn to cover them up with plausible reasons, explanations,

---

[6]Ibid., p. 196.

and justifications, all designed to "prove" that they acted in a well-thought-out and logical manner. There is a word that explains this thinking process—*rationalization*. The dictionary defines rationalization as attributing one's acts, opinions, or decisions to creditable (or reasonable) motives without analyzing the true motives. We all need to appear as "rational creatures." Employees must satisfy in their own minds that their behavior is appropriate and justified. When employees exhibit behaviors that cause conflicts, they need to be able to explain their behavior. Strong emotional wants and desires do in fact influence most employees' decisions. But most employees don't like to admit this to themselves, much less to you.

The challenge of addressing negative statements, which cause conflict, then, is learning how to make them lose force without making employees lose face. This is best done by asking nonthreatening questions that help you better understand the meaning of your employees' negative statements. You must continuously encourage your employees to demonstrate behaviors and make statements that are a true reflection of what they are thinking and feeling. You can encourage them to give you examples that better illustrate their point of view. Finally, you should encourage them to discuss in greater detail their perspective so that you can sort out their meaning more clearly. An excellent example of this technique is, "That is an interesting point, tell me more about it."

When you have learned how to listen, share, and clarify, you will be able to manage your employees' immature negative statements. You will have helped your employees to become open-minded and willing to listen. You will have recreated a positive communications climate and cleared the way to resolving the conflict.

## Problem Solving with Employees

Once you have clarified a negative statement, you are ready for the third step: actually resolving the conflict using key information and evidence. Four guidelines are useful at this step of the conflict resolution process. First, state your point of view briefly. It is important to keep your statements and opinions brief in order to maximize participation. Second, avoid using loaded words, ones that can rekindle the emotional fire still smoldering inside your employees. Third, don't withhold important information. People sometimes hold back essential information in tense times. It will not help resolve the conflict. State the truth; say what you mean and mean what you say. In other words, tell your employees exactly what you're thinking without becoming too emotional or aggressive. Fourth, disclose your feelings. Conflicts can stir up some feelings of anger or resentment. Be honest; confess them and deal with them.

We believe that by briefly stating your own views, needs, and feelings you can resolve most conflicts. The remaining part of problem solving is mutually working out solutions to your employees' concerns.

### Confirming the Answer

When a resolution is reached, you must make certain that your employees are committed to taking action to remedy the conflict. This is best accomplished by asking for some kind of immediate action. This is the final step in the conflict resolution process. It is no more difficult than that.

## USING THE CONFLICT RESOLUTION METHOD

There are four ways of using the conflict resolution method. First, you can use it when your employees are not using it. By listening, sharing, clarifying, problem solving, and confirming action, you can help your employees to simmer down and engage in a more productive discussion.

When you are involved in a dispute or sense a conflict brewing, you can overview the method briefly and ask your employees to join you in trying this way of resolving your differences. This may prevent conflicts from getting started and is an excellent way of demonstrating respect for your employees; it will help you maintain a positive relationship with them.

You can use this method to help other managers and employees resolve their conflicts. If they agree, you can serve in a third-party role as moderator. Your job is to remain neutral and make certain that the conflict resolution method is followed. Another modification of this approach is to explain the four-step process and secure the agreement of all parties to use it. Then you facilitate the process, primarily reminding them to follow the process so that they don't slip back into other ways of interacting.

One of the best ways of using the conflict resolution method is to train other managers and employees how to use it. Training classes can be set up to explain the four steps and to provide all participants an opportunity to practice using the method. Follow-up training should be used to help you and your employees transfer this method to the job. You should also maintain accurate records of how the conflict resolution method was used and how it helped resolve conflicts.

Using the conflict resolution method can foster a positive communications climate and encourage cooperation and effective working relationships. It can also help you prevent the emotional explosions that can ruin relationships and create distrust and disharmony between you and your employees.

Another outcome is that you can change the way you handle conflicts. This can dramatically improve your interactions with your employees and help them accept your ideas, constructive criticism, and corrective statements. The end result will be that your employees accept what you have to say and apply it. When this happens, their performance will improve and quality will be enhanced.

The conflict resolution method may help your employees relate to each other better. This can improve their interactions and enhance their relationships. Cooperation, trust, harmony, and teamwork will improve.

Using the conflict resolution method to handle conflicts will deepen and enrich "self-esteeming relationships." Most relationships that fail do so because the individuals in them don't know how to handle the differences between them. To ignore the differences is to resign yourselves to a superficial relationship. To fight over differences using destructive methods causes emotional explosions and hurt feelings. The conflict resolution method allows you to work through your differences so that you and your employees can better understand each other and guarantee a positive relationship.

## COLLABORATIVE PROBLEM-SOLVING PROCESS

When there is a conflict of need, the conflict resolution method is too simplistic. You must engage in collaborative problem solving to determine the best solution to the discrepancy that exists. The process consists of seven steps: problem identification, solution identification, solution analysis, solution selection, implementation of the solution, evaluation of the solution, and follow-up.[7] These steps are presented in a flowchart format in Figure 8.1.

### Problem Identification

The problem-solving process begins with identifying the expectations of the organization and comparing them to actual performance. You should analyze the current situation to determine if there is a difference between actual performance and desired performance. The discrepancy between these two positions is the "problem" facing the organization. The focus of the collaborative problem-solving process is finding the "best" solution to the

---

[7]J.W. Gilley and A.J. Coffern, *Internal Consulting for HRD Professionals: Tools, Techniques, and Strategies for Improving Organizational Performance* (Burr Ridge, IL: Irwin Professional Publishing, 1994), pp. 173–75.

**FIGURE 8.1**
*Collaborative Problem-Solving Process*

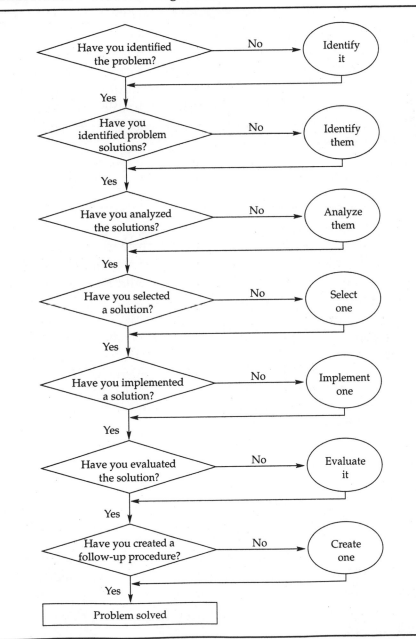

problem. During this phase, you can identify the proper actions to close the gap between expectations and actual performance.

### Solution Identification

During this phase, you should brainstorm with others to generate as many ideas as possible to identify a solution to the selected problem. This activity should be conducted without evaluating or examining the ideas. The goal is to come up with as many potential solutions as possible.

### Solution Analysis

Once all the possible solutions have been identified, you and your employees can analyze each one. Set up criteria to serve as a standard or benchmark by which to filter each idea. Ideas that meet most of the criteria are grouped together for further analysis. Ideas that don't meet the established criteria should be filed for future consideration.

### Solution Selection

Test the solutions that meet the criteria to decide their practicality and ease of application. Identify the cost and potential results of each solution. This process will help you decide which of the possible solutions are best.

Another critical part of the solution selection phase is to identify possible barriers that may prevent you from applying a solution. As these barriers are identified, look at them to decide their possible effects on various solutions. Identify actions to overcome barriers, examining financial, human, and emotional costs. This information will help you decide the best solution.

The expected outcome of this phase of the collaborative problem-solving process is that you will have identified the best alternative(s). Now senior management and you have an approach to follow in your quest to improve employee and organizational performance.

## Implementation of the Solution

During the implementation phase, the focus is on testing the solution(s) to determine its (their) results. When doing this, choose a group of employees with whom the solution has an opportunity for the highest degree of success. This strategy allows you to integrate the solution under the best possible conditions before you apply it to the entire department or division.

Implementing solutions should be a slow and deliberate process to give you time to figure out the "real" outcomes. It is often a good idea to implement a solution in several parts of an organization before introducing it to the entire organization. Then you can refine and redesign the solution as needed.

## Evaluation of the Solution

Once you have applied a solution in some proper setting, you may then gather and compare the results. If the solution helps close the gap between expectations and performance, it can be considered a success. If, however, the gap remains the same, you may need to consider alternative solutions.

Regardless of the success or failure of a solution, the information and knowledge you gain from carrying it out is valuable. This value should be communicated to others in the organization to help them improve their understanding of future performance problems.

Document the outcome of every solution tried, and keep an active record of the dates and locations of each one. This information will be an invaluable resource for future problem-solving efforts.

## Follow-Up

Follow-up is the last step in the collaborative problem-solving process. It is often the most overlooked and underestimated part of decision making. But it's the step that allows you to gather accurate information about the solutions you implement and senior management's reaction to those solutions.

You can use one-on-one personal interviews, focus groups, informal discussions, questionnaires, and reports and records to gather information about your solution(s). Employees should participate in information gathering and collection. You should analyze the findings and report them to your employees as well as to senior management.

*Chapter Nine*

# The Manager as Mentor

*The Performance Coaching Process*

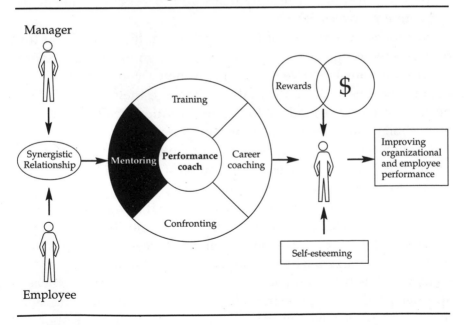

Manager

Synergistic Relationship

Employee

Mentoring

Training

Performance coach

Career coaching

Confronting

Rewards  $

Improving organizational and employee performance

Self-esteeming

The final performance coaching role is that of mentor. The role of mentor differs greatly from the other three roles (trainer, career coach, confronter) because you and your employees benefit from the relationship. The most critical outcome of mentoring is that your relationship with your employees flourish. Mentoring allows performance coaches, who have progressed in their career, to share their experiences with their employees and to help them attain the same level of success.

Why is it so important to be a mentor? Mentoring allows your employees to benefit from your experience. This includes your successes and failures. Mentoring forces you to listen attentively to the fears, concerns, frustrations, and pains as well as the successes, joys, victories, and fulfillments of your employees. Mentoring can help you become a caring, sympathetic, and patient performance coach, one who is willing to share insights and experiences with employees. In short, mentoring helps you to develop while helping your employees develop.

Mentoring is a process of ultimate sharing. It provides you the opportunity to unlock the mysteries of the organization and share them with your employees. Mentoring helps your employees to avoid mistakes and pitfalls that can damage their career. It also helps your employees adjust to the organization's culture and better assimilate into the organizational environment.

Much has been written about the difficulties of managers mentoring their own employees. Critics suggest that mentoring forces managers to choose between the interests of the organization and those of their employees. They say that this affects managers' objectivity and places them in a compromising position, making it impossible for them to "manage" their employees. The truth is that traditional managers who maintain an authoritarian, noninvolved style, which is based on the "I'm the boss—you're the employee" approach, will have an extremely difficult time performing as a mentor. However, we believe the success of any organization is based on the success of its employees, and performance coaches are the key to producing successful employees. We believe that traditional managers can't be mentors, but that performance coaches, who value the relationship they have with their employees and strive to overcome managerial malpractice, can. We believe that performance coaches who develop a synergistic, self-esteeming relationship with their employees, which is essential for a manager–employee mentoring relationship, can excel as mentors.

## ORGANIZATIONAL BENEFITS OF MENTORING

Mentoring relationships can help improve productivity by enhancing the performance of employees and teams. This is accomplished when performance coaches share with their employees how essential discipline and hard work are in succeeding within the organization. Mentoring also allows you to emphasize the importance of teamwork in overall professional success. Once they understand the need for discipline and teamwork, employees will typically improve their motivation toward their careers, which may lead to better performance and greater productivity.

When managers and employees take the opportunity to discuss important issues and topics openly, they come to understand and appreciate each other's perspective and point of view. This helps foster trust and honesty, and provides an atmosphere of sharing. The final result will be improved communications between managers and employees, which is one of the real tangible benefits of mentoring in organizations.

Over time, many managers have difficulty maintaining enthusiasm for their work and the organization. The "fires and ambitions" of their youth have dissipated. Now, their once exciting and promising career is merely a job, something to do, somewhere to go before retirement. This pervasive attitude can tear the heart out of an organization. It can kill productivity and quality. But mentoring provides tired, disenchanted, and bored managers the opportunity to guide their employees through the perils of organizational life like a lighthouse that shines the way for ships at night, steering them away from danger. Mentoring can rekindle managers' passions for their careers, which will enhance overall organizational performance.

Human resources have become an important ingredient to the long-range success of organizations. Careful planning is required to make certain that the right number of people will be available when the organization is considering its future options. Mentoring can be used as a tool to improve strategic and succession planning, which is essential for organizations to remain competitive.

Organizations also need a long-term approach in preparing for the future retirement of its employees, as well as growth and expansion opportunities. Sam Cissell, a senior manager for Cincinnati based Rogers Jewlelers, Ltd, believes that mentoring can be used as a career development tool for employees and as a career management process for organizations. She believes that together, managers and employees can develop an organizational career development system that helps the organization structure its training and development efforts, identify critical performance areas, develop career paths for all employees, establish future human resource priorities, and identify future human resource needs. All of this can be accomplished through mentoring.

## QUALIFICATIONS OF A MENTOR

Several skills, abilities, and attributes are required for managers to become effective mentors. Each of these must be developed prior to serving in the mentoring role. To effectively perform as a mentor, you must have excellent interpersonal skills. You should enjoy being with people and interacting with your employees. This will help you build a network that employees can use to learn about the organization. Mastery of the nine relationship components we discussed in Chapter Five is also essential.

An extensive knowledge of the organization is another important attribute in becoming a good mentor. The more you know about the vision, direction, and long-range goals of the organization, the better. Such organizational insight can help your employees develop political savvy and awareness as well as an understanding and appreciation of the specific nature of the organization's culture.

Mentors must have the technical competence necessary to help their employees overcome skills deficiencies, which will enable them to perform adequately within the organization. Because developing your employees is as much an act of training as it is mentoring, it is essential that you possess appropriate technical skills that will enable your employees to grow and develop.

Managers who have charisma are very successful as mentors. Why is this true? Because employees are drawn to individuals who possess the ability to persuade others and want to be around people whose opinions and ideas are sought by other members of the organization.

Mentors must also have credibility within the organization. If you're not credible, your employees will neither seek nor want your advice. One of the best ways to develop credibility as a performance coach is to make certain that you delegate work appropriately; provide specific, clear, and timely performance feedback; observe and evaluate employees' performance; help employees identify work objectives; and demonstrate acceptable professional behavior.

Finally, to be an effective mentor, you must be willing to be responsible for someone else's growth and development. At the heart of a mentoring relationship is an eagerness to improve your employees and help them become the best they can be. In fact, the very best performance coaches are comfortable and secure with letting their employees advance beyond their level. This truly demonstrates an outstanding people development philosophy.

## ACTIVITIES OF MENTORS

As mentors, performance coaches provide several activities that enhance the integrity of the relationship they have with their employees:

- Serving as a confidant in times of personal and professional problems.
- Providing feedback on observed performance.

- Providing information about the mission, goals, and strategic direction of the organization.
- Developing the political awareness and savvy of employees.
- Providing employees with insights into the organizational philosophy.
- Teaching employees how to function within the organization.
- Helping employees with long-term career planning.
- Advocating for growth opportunities.
- Encouraging risk taking.
- Providing advancement opportunities.
- Encouraging involvement in visible projects and programs.
- Serving as an honest, open, and direct adviser.

These activities are essential to the success of the mentor in performance coaching.

## BENEFITS AND PAYOFFS FOR MENTORS

Mentoring can be a very rewarding experience. You can greatly improve your interpersonal skills through effective interaction with your employees. By helping your employees grow and develop, you can enhance your self-esteem. In addition, you may be admired, respected, and noticed in the organization as a result of your mentoring activities.

By helping to develop future leaders of the organization, some performance coaches receive enhanced status in the organization, while others receive psychological rewards by simply helping other people. On occasion, you can advance your career because you're seen as a person who is very effective in developing others.

One of the biggest payoffs to the mentoring role is that it can increase your motivation and enthusiasm toward your career. This is accomplished through becoming involved with your employees and helping them walk a similar path to your own. This will help rekindle your passions for your career mission. It will also help you realize that all the effort and sacrifice has been worthwhile. Finally, mentoring may help you influence the mission and direction of the organization, which could enhance your position in the organization; you may receive recognition of your efforts from your boss or from senior management.

## ACTIVITIES OF EMPLOYEES IN MENTORING

Employees should be responsible for several activities in order for mentoring to be successful:

- Assuming responsibility for their own growth and development.
- Assessing their potential for success within the organization.
- Being receptive to positive as well as negative feedback.
- Accepting challenging assignments.
- Sharing personal information with their superior.
- Accepting suggestions and advice from another person.
- Relinquishing some control over their career path.
- Trusting the suggestions of others.

## ELEVEN STEPS IN CREATING A MENTORING RELATIONSHIP

We have developed an 11-step process to help you develop a mentoring relationship with your employees. The success of your role as mentor will depend on how well you master these steps.

### Step 1: Creating a Network

Throughout your organization there most likely are individuals you have developed relationships with who can help your employees gain much-needed knowledge about such things as the organization's history, philosophy, mission, structure, goals and objectives, and strategic direction. Hopefully, you have created such a network of individuals from a variety of departments, divisions, job functions, and managerial levels. This should provide your employees with diverse perspectives of the organization. Developing a homogeneous network can be detrimental because it will not provide your employees with a myriad of perspectives. In contrast, a heterogeneous network will increase your employees' understanding of the organization.

You may be wondering if newcomers to the organization should be included in your network. Absolutely, because these people have an opportunity to share a different organizational perspective with your employees, which will deepen their understanding of how other organizations operate. In addition, they have an opportunity to share a fresh perspective of the organization before they become totally indoctrinated.

### Step 2: Allowing Freedom

One of the drawbacks of mentoring your own employees is that they may never be exposed to different values, beliefs, and goals. Therefore, it is possible to restrict the growth and development of your employees by not allowing them to select another manager to mentor them. You may need to help some of your employees select a mentor who will challenge them.

Several years ago, we observed an interesting mentoring example. A new salesperson was working with a senior sales manager. He enjoyed watching the senior sales manager in action and felt that she would make a great mentor, because he admired her style and recognized that they had the same values and beliefs. A few months later, the rookie couldn't understand why his sales started falling when he began using the same "successful" selling techniques as the sales manager. Finally, the rookie asked another, more experienced salesperson for some feedback, and was quite surprised at what he found out. What neither he nor the senior sales manager had realized was that they were working similar territories but with very different clientele. Therefore, the techniques were inappropriate for his market. The rookie was using the wrong techniques with his customers.

The key to a successful mentoring relationship is for your employees to find someone who understands their values, beliefs, and goals, and who is willing to challenge them to succeed. Mentors should not be selected because your employees are impressed by their style.

If your employees decide to select a mentor other than you, that person should meet the same qualifications as you. We discussed the qualifications earlier in this chapter. If the potential mentor fails to meet these criteria, help your employees find a different mentor, one who shares a common understanding and language with your employees and who wants to help them grow and develop.

### Step 3: Investing Your Time Wisely

You want your employees to have a positive experience as a result of mentoring. At the same time, you want to invest your time in employees who are willing to assume responsibility for their own growth and development, who are receptive to positive and negative feedback, and who are willing to accept suggestions and advice.

Within every organization there are employees who are on the fast track to organizational success. We will call these employees fast-trackers. They help make organizations stronger and healthier through their respective tenure. They light up the room with their positive attitude and perspective. Fast-trackers are willing to learn and are receptive to positive and negative feedback. They are willing to try something new. If they fail, they view it as a learning experience. They make things happen, they are self-starters, and they take the bull by the horns—in other words, they do everything humanly possible to make things work out.

Disenchanted employees, on the other hand, tend to focus on the negative aspects of their situation. It seems that they never have anything good to say about the organization, its employees, or their job. Disenchanted employees tend to whine that nothing ever changes, but they make no attempt to help the situation. When you're around them, your energy level may drastically decline because they are constantly saying or doing something that reduces your self-esteem. They can ultimately affect your attitude, and so they're a waste of your time. You will find little joy or fulfillment in trying to mentor disenchanted employees.

You must avoid spending your valuable time trying to "save" disenchanted employees. You do have an obligation to them and to the organization to provide training, career coaching, and performance confronting. Remember, they are still employed by the organization and you have a responsibility to coach their performance. However, a negative mentoring experience will undermine all your other performance coaching efforts.

You should instead spend your time mentoring fast-trackers. They are the future leaders of the organization. Mentoring this type of employee is a good use of your time and effort. It will pay dividends and help you improve organizational performance.

### Step 4:  Giving It Away to Get It

Employees are looking for a mentor who is willing to share his or her experiences with them—a person who is willing to share equally in their successes and failures so they can grow and develop. Employees don't want a mentor who just rattles off all his or her accomplishments but rather a real human being who understands their struggles and frustrations—one who has experienced failure but has been able to overcome adversity successfully.

Dealing with failure successfully, and learning to grow from it, is what separates the fast-trackers from the disenchanted. Failure should be a learning experience, not a defining moment. It should help you discover things about yourself and make you strong, like tempered steel.

An organization that does not allow failure is an organization that will never operate at full capacity. It will be an organization that always strives for mediocrity. In contrast, allowing failure to be a learning experience will increase your employees' self-esteem, performance, and efficiency. As a mentor, you must motivate, develop, and engage your employees. You must be willing to let your employees succeed and not make the same mistakes that you and others have made. When an employee fails, you must help him or her turn the failure into a growth opportunity designed to make him or her a better person as well as employee.

Mentoring is a reciprocal process. In other words, you may gain just as much as your employees from a mentoring relationship. You learn from the process and gain valuable insights and knowledge about yourself and how to avoid making the same mistakes again. Remember, the second half of the phrase "giving it away to get it" is "to get it." This means that when you share your experiences and knowledge, you get much more in return. True mentoring is a self-esteeming process.

### Step 5: Developing Patience

"Patience is a virtue." "To learn patience you must wait." These were some of the statements you heard growing up, and they probably drove you crazy. You may have asked yourself, Why should I have to wait? Things are supposed to come to me quickly, right? Wrong! The best mentoring relationships are those that develop slowly and are based on self-esteeming principles.

What do we mean by patience? As we discussed in Chapter Five, building a relationship is a process that goes through nine distinct stages. Moving from one stage to another happens gradually. The mentoring relationship is the most fully developed and complicated relationship you will experience. It is also the most complex of all the performance coaching roles. As a result, a mentoring relationship must take its time in developing. This is where patience comes into play. The mentoring relationship must develop slowly over time because both managers and employees must feel that they are benefiting. This can only be accomplished if you have the patience to let things develop naturally.

## Step 6: Using Active Listening to Enhance Mentoring Relationships

As a mentor, you must have the ability to successfully and patiently listen to your employees' needs. Their needs should be your primary focus. In Chapter Seven, we examined how active listening can help you be a more successful career coach. Active listening is a skill that enables you to build a more productive and beneficial relationship with your employees. The same benefits exist when you use active listening to foster a mentoring relationship with your employees.

One thing that may be of interest to you is that listeners:

**L**ook
**I**nterested
**S**o
**T**o
**E**ngage
**N**onverbally
**E**mpathically and
**R**espectively

We believe that this acrostic will help you recall and apply the behaviors of an effective listener.

## Step 7: Having Chemistry

When you are in the process of building a mentoring relationship, one of the most important steps is having chemistry with your employees. We believe some type of "deep connection" should exist between the two of you. If it does not exist, maybe a mentoring relationship is not advisable. We have had managers and employees tell us that the chemistry that exists in a mentoring relationship is much deeper than anything else they have experienced in a work setting. Some have shared with us that it is a kind of "spiritual" connection. They tell us that through this connection a deeper level of understanding exists that truly allows self-esteeming to flourish.

During a management development program that we conducted, the issue of mentoring was brought up. As the discussion deepened, one of the participants said to another, "You know what? You and I have this kind of relationship." We asked them to tell us about the most important part of their relationship, and they both agreed: It was the chemistry that existed between them. It allowed them both to learn and grow from each other. What was very interesting was that neither person had ever discussed the word *mentoring* prior to this program. This demonstrates that many mentoring relationships are often informal, unstructured experiences.

### Step 8: Formally Establishing a Mentoring Relationship

Many of you have mentoring relationships that you're not aware of. How can this happen? Over time, you develop healthy relationships with a variety of employees that fall somewhere in the relationship model. The closer they get to the self-esteeming and personal development component, the more they have evolved into a mentoring relationship. However, formally structuring a mentoring relationship can add a great deal of impact. For example, you may become a better listener or become more patient. Most important, you realize the gravity of the relationship and the responsibility it brings. This will help you become more responsive to the needs of your employees, which will enable you to enhance your involvement in their development.

Formalizing mentoring enables you to create a development plan with each employee that will serve as a contract between you and the employee. It outlines your respective responsibilities; the specific goals and outcomes your employee wants to achieve; action steps and strategies that will be used to accomplish the goals and outcomes; target dates for the completion of each action step; and resource requirements such as people, funds, and other items needed to execute the agreement. A mentoring plan should also include a section where you identify the progress and status of each action step used by your employee (see Figure 9.1). A

**FIGURE 9.1**
*Sample Mentoring Plan*

| Name ——————————————— |  |  |  |
| Date ——————————————— |  |  |  |

*Goal/Outcome*

| *Action/Steps* | *Target Date* | *Resource Required* | *Status/Progress* |
|---|---|---|---|
|  |  |  |  |

mentoring plan serves as a road map for the development of your employees. Once a mentoring plan has been negotiated, you know which activities and what kind of training you will perform. It motivates you to do a good job and helps you stay focused.

When you formalize a mentoring relationship, your employees may feel quite relieved because all the cards are on the table. In our example, the employee said that it was funny because she felt that a great weight was lifted from her shoulder and she believed that their relationship could get even better and more self-esteeming.

Going public with your mentoring relationship establishes a developmental contract between you and your employees, which can help structure activities, training, and discussions. However, one of the main reasons why mentoring relationships remain informal and unspoken is that employees fear rejection. They also fear that the relationship will change if it becomes formal. We asked the employee in our example why she had never formally asked her manager to be a mentor. She replied, "I didn't want anything to get in the way of the relationship."

The easiest way to establish a formal mentoring relationship is to encourage your employees to ask a manager (or you) to be their mentor. That's right—your employees have to take a risk, and ask. What your employees don't realize is that future mentors need the validation as much as they need someone to help them grow and develop. If they don't ask, they will miss a developmental opportunity of a lifetime.

### Step 9: Establishing Relationship Boundaries

Boundaries are critical in a mentoring relationship. They are formal lines drawn in the sand that define the relationship. Boundaries help you and your employees feel more comfortable during mentoring. Usually boundaries develop informally. They begin to become apparent when you start to get to know someone on a personal level. This is not to say that boundaries do not begin earlier, because they exist in every relationship from the very beginning. However, once you begin to interact on a personal level, you discover what you can and cannot discuss with another person.

Some employees are very open and are willing to share their thoughts and feelings, while others are very controlled and closed. The latter will have difficulty sharing their thoughts and feelings with you.

The taboo topics can include, but are not limited to, workplace issues. Such topics as reporting relationships, peer-to-peer relationships, and promotions may be considered off-limits. In order to develop trust and honesty, you must set boundaries; otherwise, things may be discussed and passed on that are inappropriate. Boundaries have to be set based on reciprocity. Managers and employees must make clear what can and cannot be discussed.

In some mentoring relationships, boundaries may be a little more relaxed because there is not a reporting relationship. A non-reporting relationship allows you to stretch the boundaries because performance and productivity are not at risk.

## Step 10:  Creating Relationship Reciprocity

Mentoring relationships must be reciprocal. If they are not, self-esteeming does not occur, which means that the interaction is nothing more than a working relationship. While a positive working relationship is critical to the success of all organizations, it is not enough for mentoring to be successful. Mentoring must be two-way in order for both parties to benefit. In reciprocal relationships, managers and employees grow and learn from one another. It is true that your employees may benefit the most from mentoring, but you too will learn and grow.

## Step 11:  Developing Synergy

Once you have developed the first 10 steps, you are at a point where the relationship has gone "outside the box." Not only is self-esteeming happening on a regular basis, but synergy is now an everyday occurrence. Synergy occurs when the whole is greater than the sum of the parts. In other words, the sum of the mentoring relationship is bigger than the people involved. Think of the best working relationship you have ever had with someone. Wouldn't you say that while you were in the relationship you were more creative, innovative, spontaneous, and productive, and that your self-esteem was more positive than before you were involved? This is what we mean by "synergistic relationships."

We experienced synergy while writing this book. The more we interacted and discussed ideas and approaches, the more we were able to challenge each other. As a result, we believe we created a much better book together than we could have separately. This is the beauty of a synergistic relationship.

Mentoring in its truest sense is self-esteeming and synergistic. Mentoring allows you and your employees to feed off each other, which creates reciprocal self-esteem. A synergistic relationship allows you and your employees to think outside the box.

### *Author Tribute*

While writing this book, we observed a manager who demonstrated exceptional mentoring skills. Her example was an inspiration to us and we would like to recognize **Sam Cissell** of Rogers Jewelers, Ltd., for her insights, abilities, skills, and dedication to developing her employees. Her example is refreshing. We thank her for her openness, honesty, and willingness to develop others.

*Chapter Ten*

# Developing Self-Esteeming Employees and Teams

*The Performance Coaching Process*

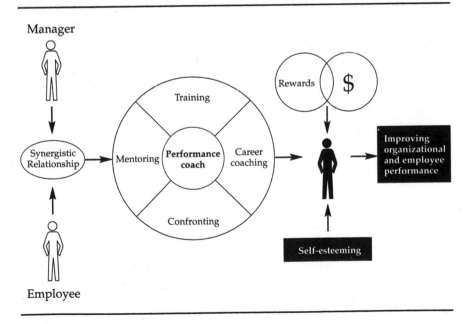

In this book we have defined *self-esteeming* as a synergistic relationship between you and your employees where you feed off each other, a relationship where the whole is greater than the sum of its parts. Self-esteeming is also based on an enormously powerful need to feel good about yourself and your experiences, skills, and abilities. In short, self-esteeming is the sum total of how you feel about yourself.

We believe that the primary outcome of the performance coaching process is self-esteeming. It is based on collegial partnerships between you and your employees. We discussed in Chapter Five that this partnership is based on two-way communications, trust, honesty, and interaction, and that it should be nonjudgmental, fear-free, personal, and professionally developmental. Self-esteeming provides you an opportunity to better serve your employees through training, career coaching, confronting, and mentoring. These roles help your employees improve their personal self-esteem, which will result in better organizational performance.

In addition, self-esteeming is an approach that helps you benefit by increasing your involvement with your employees. This can help energize you and keep you engaged in challenging projects, activities, and growth opportunities. Self-esteeming can help you grow and develop because you will be more encouraged to tackle increasingly difficult assignments. You will also begin to initiate changes that will improve your employees and the organization.

Your self-concept is the "net balance" of your experiences, positive and negative. When your self-concept is essentially positive, you feel alive and able to take risks, to listen, to grow, to be unique and expressive, to care, and to be courageous—in a word, to be and become whatever is in you. When your self-concept is basically negative, you are defensive and frightened; you tend to become closed to experiences, to distrust others, to avoid conflict, to stop growing, and to retreat.

Self-esteeming is what is put into or taken out of your self-concept, its building up or its tearing down. Self-esteeming is a bit like credits and debits: The net balance is what you experience; it is what you feel about yourself. Self-esteeming, then, is the net of your experiences and may lead either to a more positive or a more negative self-concept.

## EMPOWERMENT FAILURE

One of the enemies of self-esteeming is the empowerment fad. Empowerment is based on the belief that you can provide your employees the "power" to become more responsible or achieve greater levels of performance. While the outcomes are appealing, the concept is based on the same old managerial paradigm that has been in existence for hundreds of years.

The empowerment movement is based mainly on power and control. For example, let's imagine that, as a manager, you "empower" an employee to take on greater responsibility. What you're really saying is that *you* are granting the employee the right to take on greater responsibility. The power resides within you. In other words, it's your power you're giving away and with no strings attached. What is wrong with this? At first glance it looks like a good approach, but further examination reveals its fatal flaws.

First, as a manager you cannot grant power to another person. Power resides within each individual employee. In an employer–employee relationship it's the employee who allows the employer to manage him or her. That's right, your employees allow you to be the manager. Think about it. If your employees collectively decided to refuse to let you manage them, what could you do about it? You could fire them, yes. What else could you do? Nothing. That is all you could do. But you haven't managed them. Where is your so-called power to manage and get things done? You're helpless. Let us repeat: All managers are granted the right to manage by their employees. This right is not given to you by upper management. It's given to you by your employees. So you can't empower your employees because they already have the power inside themselves. Your primary objective is to get your employees to realize that they have the power inside them to achieve great things and to get the results you want. The sooner you understand this basic premise, the better performance coach you will become.

Second, empowerment is based on granting control to your employees. Again, do you have any control to grant? The answer is no. You may think you do because you can hire and fire your employees; and you can promote and advance them. What else can you control? Not very much. Your employees have majority ownership of control in managerial situations. You can't possibly control your employees unless they allow you to do so. Think about it. How can you control the thoughts, actions, or behaviors of 10, 20, 30, or more employees? You can't. Your employees must be willing to abide by the established rules and regulations. Otherwise, chaos will prevail. You can't force them to do anything they don't want to do. You have only one recourse. You must gain and maintain your employees' respect in order for them to grant you the right to control.

Third, empowerment is a one-way process from manager to employee. Empowerment continues to reinforce the authoritarian manager model that it is trying to replace. Your employees aren't stupid. They know what's going on. They know you're still "telling" them what to do; you've just changed your approach. Where is the *internal* motivation that empowerment is supposed to produce? It is not there because a one-way process is self-serving and is not designed to produce a synergistic outcome.

Finally, your employees are the only ones who would benefit from a one-way process of empowerment. You don't benefit from empowerment. Empowerment, if it works at all, doesn't help you improve your internal motivation or self-esteem. Empowerment is simply another way to get work accomplished by your employees. It does have value, but it has serious limitations in getting the most out of your employees while enhancing their self-esteem.

In summary, empowerment doesn't work because it is based on two things you can't delegate to your employees (because they already possess them): power and control. It also fails because it is a one-way process instead of a reciprocal one.

## OPPORTUNITIES FOR SELF-ESTEEMING

Employees interact with their environment every day, which gives managers an opportunity to enhance or diminish their self-esteem. Their interactions can include you, other employees, other managers, projects, activities, assignments, meetings, situations, presentations, and/or proposals. Together these interactions make up your employees' "private and public world," a world you can draw from to bolster your employees' self-esteem. The same world, however, can deplete their self-esteem through negative experiences, causing them to feel depressed, hurt, and angry.

### *Sources of Self-Esteem*

There are many sources of self-esteem you can draw from to improve your employees' overall self-concept. The four primary sources are the following:

- Achievement, accomplishment, and mastery.
- Power, control, and influence.
- Being cared about and valued.
- Acting on values and beliefs.

Each of these sources serves as a conduit from your employees' experiences (world) to their overall self-esteem level (see Figure 10.1). The four sources of self-esteem enable positive experiences to flow into your employees' "self-concept bucket." The more positive experiences your employees have, the higher their self-esteem level will become. In other words, the higher their self-esteem level, the greater their self-concept will be.

Over time, your employees' self-esteem level begins to evaporate and is in need of being replenished. If positive experiences don't continue to occur, your employees can't refill their self-esteem level and it begins to go down. The net effect is a lower self-concept. During this period your employees may be easily hurt and angry, may take few risks, and may not listen. Therefore, you must find ways to refill your employees' self-concept buckets. This

**FIGURE 10.1**
*Sources of Self-Esteem*

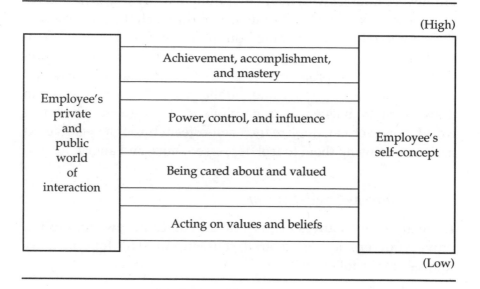

can best be done by using one or all of the four sources of self-esteem: achievement, accomplishment and mastery; power, control, and influence; being cared about and valued; and acting on values and beliefs.

**Achievement, accomplishment, and mastery.**    All of your employees need opportunities to achieve or accomplish something that is meaningful to them. Being creative, acquiring new knowledge, and challenging themselves intellectually are all activities that can help your employees enhance their self-esteem. But for achievement and accomplishment to have a real impact, you must encourage your employees to set recognizable goals. By doing this, they will "own" the goal personally. Reaching some goal set by you is not nearly as satisfying or esteem-producing as reaching ones they establish for themselves.

To enhance self-esteem, a goal should be attainable, neither so easy that it is not a challenge nor so difficult that success is essentially impossible. The goal doesn't need to be large, important, or visible to others, but simply personally owned, challenging, and satisfying. Therefore, your employees will receive something intrinsically valuable upon completion.

Mastery is another excellent way of enhancing your employees' self-esteem. By mastery we mean any activity that your employees can accomplish at the highest possible performance level. Normally, this involves using strength or a combination of the strengths we discussed in Chapter Four. Mastery brings the highest level of personal satisfaction to your employees, which greatly enhances their self-esteem.

In order to gain maximum self-esteem from an activity, your employees need to receive regular and timely feedback regarding their performance. There is little satisfaction and self-esteem growth unless your employees get feedback on how they are doing on a regular basis and immediately after the result has been achieved.

In summary, your employees' self-esteem can increase dramatically through achievement, accomplishment, and mastery. But to be really effective, goals that are identified must be personally owned; they should be challenging yet attainable; and there should be relatively immediate and clear feedback about how successful your employees have been.

**Power, control, and influence.**   In organizations there is nothing more demeaning—or such a source of anger and frustration—than having something of significance happen to you for which you had no input, no influence, and no control. It discounts you, diminishes your worth, undercuts your effectiveness, degrades you as a human being, and renders you powerless. This is why announcements of an organizational change sometimes lead to open conflict and sullen hostility, even when the imposed change is a significant improvement for the employees. Your employees' self-esteem is tied directly to the things they can influence and control. When your employees lose their power over decision making, they lose respect for themselves.

However, advancing their career, having influence over decisions, having status, having authority over others, and having power and control can greatly enhance your employees' self-esteem. Many employees identify with these traditional symbols of success and want the organization to provide them such opportunities. Employees also want the organization to reward and recognize their contributions. Such efforts help improve their self-esteem.

In many cases, you can improve your employees' self-esteem by appointing them to chair committees, task forces, and/or projects where they can have influence over the results. In other situations, you can rely on their advanced knowledge and expertise to affect the outcomes. While in other circumstances, you can depend on your employees' interpersonal persuasiveness and charisma to influence the success of a major presentation or proposal. In each case, you can use power, control, and influence as a valid source to improve self-esteem.

**Being cared about and valued.**   At an early age, people learn the importance of receiving warmth and affection from those who are important to them. In organizations, however, warmth and affection are often discounted and regarded as unimportant and insignificant. But such personal involvement is a very important source of self-esteem and should be treated accordingly. Many employees gain positive self-esteem from meaningful interpersonal contact, comfortable relationships with important individuals, and feeling a part of a group. Many employees value close personal affiliation with others within the organization. Many employees view their co-workers as members of an extended family and the organization as a meaningful family unit. Many employees personally identify with their organization and become quite emotionally attached.

In Chapter Five, we emphasized the importance of collegial partnerships as a means of demonstrating to your employees that you do care for them and value them as people. It is also a relationship that allows you to recognize your employees for their overall and specific contributions to performance improvement and organizational efficiency.

**Acting on values and beliefs.**   Most of your employees have a core set of values and beliefs that guides much of their behavior. These beliefs can serve as a source of positive self-esteem if employees are able to act consistently with them. However, the reverse is also true. When circumstances and events cause you and your employees to act counter to your deeply held values, you each feel diminished. You may not like yourself very much, and you may become depressed and angry.

Acting on your values and beliefs is not as simple as it seems. One of the most common mistakes managers make is to communicate double messages. For example, many managers encourage their employees to maintain a balance between their work and family while knowing that productivity pressures will prevent this from happening. This apparent inconsistency between what managers tell their employees and what they then demand can create serious internal value conflicts for their employees. If productivity pressures continue to prevent employees from spending an appropriate amount of time with their families, they will be forced to choose between the job and their family. This is a self-esteem killer because it is a lose–lose situation unless managers can better control the work environment and make certain that it doesn't severely interfere with their employees' values.

You must first help your employees identify and understand their values so that they have a clear picture of what's important to them. Second, values identification can help employees determine where potential conflicts might occur. Third, you should help your employees sort through conflicting values in order to limit the friction between them. By doing this, your employees will feel better about themselves and their situation.

When your employees behave in accordance with basic beliefs, they feel good about themselves. Self-esteem is increased, and the idea of who they are, their self-concept, becomes more positive and clear. Being in touch with their true feelings and having an accurate picture of themselves has a very positive effect on your employees' self-esteem.

### Results of Using Sources of Self-Esteem

When your employees experience an adequate amount of self-esteem for one or more of the four major sources, their self-concept tends to be positive. They feel good about themselves as an effective, competent, and ethical individual. Some of the resulting feelings and behaviors are listed below:

- Commitment
- Risk taking
- Trust
- Assurance
- Creativity
- Sharing

- Caring
- Openness
- Cooperation
- Uniqueness
- Listening
- Realness

- Growth
- Courage
- Candor
- Expressiveness
- Personal security
- Confrontation of conflicts

When these feelings and behaviors are present, your employees are motivated to improve their performance, help solve problems, and secure the results needed by the organization.

The reverse is also true. When work experiences produce self-esteem that is inadequate, your employees' self-concept ultimately suffers. They begin to find fault with themselves and dislike who they are. They will try to break away from depression by unconsciously striving to return to equilibrium. But in many cases it is impossible to regain their positive outlook. When this occurs they exhibit behaviors like the ones listed below:

- Low trust
- Nonlistening
- Anger, rage
- Suspicion
- Low self-esteem

- Low risk
- Low creativity
- Fearfulness
- Stagnation
- Low courage

- Conformity
- Accommodation
- Vulnerability
- Manipulation
- Sadness

Improved performance and quality can't be forthcoming from employees who possess these types of behaviors. Let's now look at the impact of high and low self-esteem on teams as well as on the organization.

## IMPACT OF SELF-ESTEEMING ON TEAMS

A team is a collection of individuals striving to accomplish predetermined goals or objectives. A team is like a person; it can have positive or negative self-esteem. Team behavior can be similar to employees' behavior previously discussed. In addition, each individual team member is positively or adversely impacted by the outcomes of the team and the interactions that occur as a result of the team's efforts.

When attempting to enhance the self-esteem of the team, you can rely on the same four sources of self-esteem used to bolster individual self-esteem. However, greater conflicts can exist among sources of self-esteem in a team setting than with individuals. For example, several team members could aggressively compete for power and influence, which can increase stress and conflict among all team members and can jeopardize achieving the team's goal. This can negatively affect all team members, not just the individuals directly involved in the struggle for power.

### The Changing Role of Team Leader

As you evolve from manager to performance coach, you build ever-greater trust among your employees. The respect you show your employees for their decisions and contributions builds their confidence, which begins to inspire teamwork. Over time, teamwork is instilled as an organizational value. Eventually, trust and teamwork help build strong employee teams. As a member of a strong team, employees can help the organization become more competitive.

As teams develop, your performance coaching role becomes one of facilitator and supporter. You lead decision-making sessions where employees work to reach consensus and develop plans of action. You will also provide resource support to help your employees implement their plans of action.

As employees become more self-esteeming, your role becomes a more strategic one. Your job now is to prepare employees to share leadership duties with you. Your mentoring, career coaching, and training activities should have prepared several employees to assume the team's leadership responsibilities. You should delegate the appropriate leadership assignments and work directly with the chosen leaders to assure a smooth transition.

## Impact of Team Development on Self-Esteeming

As the new leadership team begins to take root, you should encourage and support its development. You should rely on your mentoring and relationship skills in helping employees accept and adopt their new leadership team. You may even serve as a cheerleader for the group, providing the team an emotional boost. At this point in the team's evolution, a new identity has been born.

## Evolution of Teams

Every team goes through ups and downs before the members gel. Understanding these phases can help you and your team weather the suffering and confusion. Teams experience anticipation, anger, acceptance, and renewed confidence in roughly that order as they evolve. For each team member these emotional states produce positive and negative experiences that can affect their self-esteem.

**Forming.** In the first phase, team members are getting acquainted and starting to build a relationship. They ask questions: "What's expected of me?" "How do I fit in?" "What are we supposed to do?" "What are the rules?" They are trying to decide what behaviors are accepted, what the team task is, and how the group will go about carrying out its work. During this phase, anxiety quickly follows the initial excitement. Open conflict is rare because no one feels secure enough yet to be "real." Forming is a period of orientation and dependency, and team members look to you (the formal leader) for guidance and leadership.

The forming phase can be an excellent opportunity to develop positive self-esteem. Team members are engaged in the business of small talk and anxious enthusiasm. Your employees can get a sense of belonging and being valued during this phase as well as an opportunity to discuss and influence the values and directions of the team. All of these are excellent sources for building positive self-esteem.

**Storming.**    During the second phase, enthusiasm often gives way to frustration and anger. The storming phase is a period of conflict among team members and resistance to the task. Team members struggle to find ways to work together, and everything seems awkward. This phase is characterized by hostility among team members and toward you as a leader. There may also be some resistance to the structure of the group. Previously established ground rules may splinter like a tree in an Oklahoma tornado.

During this phase, team members are testing each other and developing a sense of boundaries and trust. The storming phase is critical because it will determine the interaction between team members and the way the team will function for the remainder of the time it is together. If a team survives this phase, it will be stronger because the sum of its parts will truly be a highly effective team.

All the self-esteeming gains made during the forming phase can be destroyed during the storming phase. Employees are at each other's throats during this period in a struggle that can be characterized as the survival of the fittest. Your role during this period is to help maintain a sense of balance and sanity. You can't allow conflicts to get out of control. The self-concept of every team member is on the line. You should rely on your assertive skills and the four-step conflict resolution method discussed in Chapter Eight to help you reduce tensions and fears.

This can be a win–lose period for the team. Some managers view the storming phase as an internal contest between team members. Someone has to win, and someone has to lose. When this attitude is present, the only losers are the team and the organization; there are no winners.

We see the storming phase as an external contest. No one wins if the team fails to achieve its objective and team members don't have a positive experience. All team members win if the team wins. The focus must be on the team's objective, not on who has power and control. When this occurs, self-esteeming is the result. All team members receive a solid dose of positive self-esteem.

**Norming.** Gradually, the team gains its balance and enters the tranquil "norming" phase. A sense of group cohesion develops. The power struggles are over, a code of conduct and behavior has been adopted, and everyone makes a conscious effort to get along. There is an increased willingness to share the work load, and information is freely shared and acted on. It's a period of openness and trust among team members.

The primary danger now is that team members hold back their good ideas for fear of further conflict. You must help the team members move through their reticence. This can be done by increasing their responsibilities and authority. Giving team members a new challenge demonstrates your trust in them. Meeting that challenge strengthens their trust in one another.

Norming is a period of rebuilding the self-esteem lost during the storming war. The team is beginning to achieve what it was commissioned to do. It's time to let employees use their expertise to demonstrate their mastery. Sharing increasing responsibilities allows team members to receive greater self-confidence, which will enhance their self-esteem.

**Performing.** During the performing phase, interpersonal relationships have been stabilized, the roles have been clarified, and the team moves toward accomplishment. Smooth self-confidence is the attitude of team members as they go about achieving the desired objective. By now, team members have learned to disagree constructively; they resolve conflicts without hurt feelings or negative consequences. The team is clearly defined and its purpose is known to all. Simply said, the team is executing to perfection.

The performing phase is characterized by results being accomplished and victories being won. Victory is so sweet. All the conflicts, disagreements, hurt feelings, and endless hours of hard work are forgotten. It's a time and place of inner peace and of personal satisfaction. There is also a sense of accomplishment but, most important, there is a feeling of wholeness. You truly feel like you're walking on air. You're above the clouds. Unfinished business has been finished.

The feeling you experience immediately after victory is what we mean by *self-esteeming*. If you could bottle this feeling and give it to your employees, you would never need to worry about performance improvement and quality again. The performance would be there. The problems would be solved, and the results would be obtained.

By recognizing the four phases of team development, you are in a better position to address the concerns of team members. Remember, the goal is to develop high-performing teams and keep them together in order to achieve the results you need.

## Self-Esteeming and Conflict Resolution

To become a totally self-esteeming team, you must anticipate possible conflicts. In order to resolve conflicts properly, you must identify and acknowledge differences among team members. You must help team members understand and accept their individual differences. This requires team members to utilize and capitalize on diverse backgrounds, viewpoints, and skills. As a performance coach, your responsibility is to mentor and counsel informal team leaders as they work with the team. You should use facilitation skills to help move the team forward.

## ORGANIZATIONAL IMPACT OF SELF-ESTEEMING

Organizations, like individuals, are a living system—and by analogy at least, the two share many processes. Organizations with low self-esteem act in a way strikingly similar to the way an individual with low self-esteem would act. That is, organizations with low self-esteem often demonstrate such feelings and behaviors as the ones listed below:

- Easily threatened
- Anger, resentment
- Autocratic managers
- Conflict avoidance

- Low creativity
- Manipulation
- Politicking
- Fear

- Blaming
- Low risk taking
- Win–lose postures
- Intragroup conflict

These feelings and behaviors inevitably result in poor performance and low self-esteeming for employees.

However, organizations with high self-esteem demonstrate behaviors almost exactly opposite to those listed. They perform very well and get the results they need. Moreover, employees receive positive self-esteem by being a part of such an organization.

Figure 10.2 illustrates how self-esteem impacts organizational performance. The four sources of self-esteem are identified on the far left. You can clearly see the results of positive and negative self-concept on the individual and the organization. If employee self-concept is positive, it results in such things as commitment, growth, openness, trust, and creativity. Organizations with high self-concept demonstrate such things as two-way communications, open confronting and conflict resolution, win–win approaches, openness and responsiveness, and high commitment to human resources. This ultimately leads to higher performance and greater employee satisfaction.

However, the opposite is true for employees and organizations with a low self-concept. Employees with a low self-concept demonstrate such things as low courage, anger, stagnation, fearfulness, and conflict avoidance. Organizations with a low self-concept produce such things as low creativity, low risk taking, win–lose

## FIGURE 10.2
### *Organizational Impact of Self-Esteem*

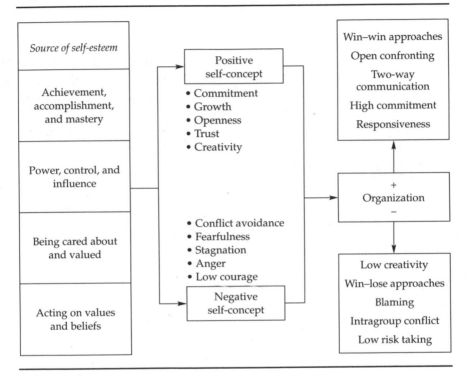

approaches, blaming, and intragroup conflict. The combination of low employee and organization self-concept leads to poor performance and low employee satisfaction.

It is difficult to improve an organization with a low self-concept. However, you can have dramatic success with the employees you are responsible for managing. Over time, your successes will have a positive impact on the organization. If a number of managers within the same organization become dedicated to self-esteeming their employees and teams, the organization will experience the results in a few short months.

## Chapter Eleven

# Getting Results through Rewards

*The Performance Coaching Process*

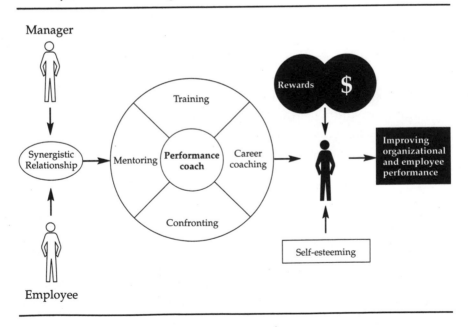

The purpose of any organization is to get results. For some organizations the desired results could include increasing market share, improving quality, increasing sales, and/or increasing profitability. Regardless, it is the responsibility of performance coaches to get the results the organization needs. But you can't do it alone. You must get results through people.

Throughout this book, we have been talking about strategies that help you get the results you want. We discussed the importance of reengineering the training function in order to improve learning transfer so that performance can improve. We suggested that training be broken down into a modularized format to enhance application. We provided strategies that would help you use your current training professionals as internal consultants responsible for performance management systems. We detailed the responsibilities of performance coaches and how each of the four roles help them solve problems and improve performance. Finally, we discussed how performance coaches could better manage teams. We would like to conclude our journey by discussing reward strategies and rewards that help you get the results you need.

You must find ways to enhance your employees' commitment through motivational strategies. We believe that there is a straightforward, commonsense approach that performance coaches should follow. You should tell your employees exactly what you expect of them. This includes telling them what results or outcomes you want, what level of quality you need, and when the results are needed. It would help employees greatly if you could provide them with performance standards to guide their efforts.

Performance standards offer an easy way for employees to monitor their own outputs and evaluate their own performance. You should communicate the importance of the outcomes they are producing. Also, tell them how their contributions affect the entire project or production. This information helps employees understand the importance of producing outcomes on time and at the proper level of quality. They also know how their efforts affect the final product.

Next, tell your employees how they are doing. Employees need timely and continuous feedback in order to remain on track. Feedback helps to motivate them and provides the information that lets them alter and improve their efforts. Finally, you must reward employees who perform well. You must establish a clear link between producing positive outcomes and having their efforts recognized. Research has shown that the things that get rewarded and reinforced will be repeated.

## PRINCIPLES OF PERFORMANCE IMPROVEMENT

Have you ever wondered why employees behave the way they do? We believe that there are three fundamental principles that explain most employee behaviors. These principles also explain why organizations don't get the results they want.

### *Disconnect Theory*

The success of today's organizations is greatly affected by the disconnect between the performance we need and the performance we reward. For example, organizations spend millions of dollars on training people in team-building skills and teamwork but continue to give bonuses and financial rewards to individual employees. In such cases, right behavior is being ignored or punished in the workplace, and wrong behavior is being rewarded. For example, does your organization:

- Ask for quality work but establish unrealistic deadlines for its completion?
- Want projects completed on time, but do nothing when a senior manager waits until the last minute to begin a project?
- Want quality solutions to problems but reward quick fixes?
- Need better results but reward those who look the busiest and work the longest hours?

Establishing the proper connection between performance and rewards is the single greatest factor to improving performance. We
believe if you reward people for the right performance, you will
get the right results. If you fail to reward the right behaviors, you
will likely get the wrong results. Said another way, "The things
that get rewarded, get done."[1]


## Expectation Theory

Fifteen years ago, we interviewed a 35-year veteran of elementary
education. We asked her to tell us the single most successful practice she used to improve student performance. She paused and
said, "The key is simple. It's not what you expect, it's what you inspect that gets results." We asked her to explain why this idea was
so successful. She added, "Young people learn at an early age that
they must choose what they are going to spend their time on, so
they choose the things that will make you the happiest. See, they
want to make you happy, they look up to you (as their teacher)
and want to please you. They think of you as a friend or parental
figure. They know that if you're going to spend time looking at
their work it must be important to you. So they spend their time
doing as good a job for you as they can. They also know the things
you don't look at must not be as important to you and that they
are less likely to be recognized for their efforts."

During the past 15 years, we have looked to see if this same
principle can be applied to employees within organizations. We
discovered that employees learn very quickly what your "hot buttons" are and they perform accordingly. They know that not all
their work is equal in importance. They will spend little time on
the jobs you don't inspect or review.

---

[1]M. LeBoeuf, *Getting Results: The Secret to Motivating Yourself and Others* (New York:
Berkley Books, 1985), p. 9.

### *Priority Theory*

Sometimes managers treat all results the same and fail to communicate which results are the most important. This can confuse employees and cause them to produce results that are of little value to the organization. If you're focusing on less important priorities, so will your employees—and you can't expect them to know the difference.

As a performance coach, you must focus on the right things. You must determine what results are really the most important. Once they have been identified, you have answered the question, "What needs to be rewarded?" In other words, once you have identified the highest priorities for the organization, you can create a reward strategy that produces those results.

## REWARD STRATEGIES THAT ENHANCE COMMITMENT AND GET RESULTS

There are four reward strategies that help performance coaches enhance employee commitment and get results: (1) rewarding long-term solutions, (2) rewarding entrepreneurship, (3) rewarding performance improvement and quality work, and (4) rewarding teamwork and cooperation.[2]

### *Strategy 1: Rewarding Long-Term Solutions*

In today's organizations, short-term rewards are often the only ones offered. Organizational leaders are under extreme pressure to produce monthly and quarterly results in order to satisfy stockholders and parent companies. Because of this emphasis, many of the decisions made ultimately hurt organizations. Organizations must begin to adopt reward strategies that help them accomplish

---

[2]Ibid., pp. 107–108.

long-term growth and development. Then and only then will the focus of organizations be on long-term rather short-term solutions.

Let's look at several examples of the differences between long-term and short-term solutions:

| Long-Term Solutions | Short-Term Solutions |
| --- | --- |
| Invest in the growth and development of a committed and dedicated workforce. | Hire and fire people as needed. |
| Focus on repeat business by improving customer service and value-added selling. | Cut prices to generate short-term revenue. |
| Emphasize quality as the key to improving productivity, products, and services. | Focus on delivering the product or service on time at any cost. |
| Develop long-term profit and loss statements. | Maintain a monthly profit and loss statement. |
| Commit to new and better products and services through innovations, research, and development. | Avoid risk taking unless the payoff is immediate. |

Performance coaches can do a number of things to encourage long-term solutions. They can give employees who successfully produce positive results long-term rewards. For example, you can give them a yearly bonus in stock credits to be redeemed at retirement. You can create a sabbatical program for employees who have long-term positive service. You can establish a compensation system tied directly to the performance, profitability, and prosperity of the organization.

## Strategy 2: Rewarding Entrepreneurship

In order to develop an ownership attitude among employees, performance coaches must develop a reward system that encourages risk taking and decisive action. If implemented, it will help foster an entrepreneurial approach to performance improvement.

When employees are encouraged to act on their convictions, positive outcomes will result. Performance coaches must allow employees to assert their point of view, and must be willing to support their assertions. It requires self-confidence for employees to tell the manager that there is a better way of getting a job done. It takes a lot of courage for employees to put their career on the line to help move the organization forward. This type of behavior should be recognized and rewarded. Success and failure often depend on the degree of risk employees are willing to take. Employees who are willing to take chances energize other employees. Such an atmosphere can help produce positive results. Organizations also promote individuals who help improve their results. This is another good reason managers should encourage their employees to take risks and decisive action.

Failure is one of the best learning experiences an employee can have. As a manager, you can let your employees experience "controlled" failure (failure without severe consequences). Don't bail them out of trouble. Help them, however, work through the feelings and emotions associated with failure to help rebuild their self-esteem and confidence.

Remember, the purpose of risk taking is to improve people and organizations, not to create foolhardy daredevils. You should teach your employees to take intelligent risks.

As a performance coach, one of your jobs is to celebrate the successes with your employees. You should also console them after their defeats and help them release the negative feelings and tensions associated with an unsuccessful venture. This will help them be more receptive to moving on to the next challenge.

### Strategy 3: Rewarding Performance Improvement and Quality Work

Improving performance appears to be a mystery to many managers. However, there are several useful actions that may help foster the performance you desire. Select the right person for the job and give them the resources to accomplish the work. By *the right person*, we mean an employee who has the training and ability to successfully complete the work. On occasion, employees with the aptitude to learn the skills can be trained to complete the work. Regardless, provide whomever you choose with the equipment, data, and time necessary to produce a quality output.

Next, communicate your expectations and a clear sense of how the job contributes to the overall work effort. People need to know what you want them to do, by when, and at what level of quality. They also need to know the importance of their personal contributions. Those employees who realize the value of their efforts are less likely to waste time on intangible activities.

You can encourage efficiency and quality by allowing employees who finish satisfactory work early some time off. Also, allow employees to remain at home to finish projects and activities whenever possible. It communicates that you have confidence in their professionalism and maturity.

Improving performance requires simplification. This includes eliminating unnecessary jobs, flattening organizational structures, reducing procedures and controls, and simplifying communications. To accomplish this, you should encourage your employees to study and review their work. You should eliminate redundant steps, replace obsolete equipment, and discover more efficient ways of producing products or services. Once you have identified economies, you should develop and adopt improved methods. Employees should then be rewarded for their contributions and efforts.

### Strategy 4: Rewarding Teamwork and Cooperation

Many organizations talk about the importance of teamwork and cooperation. However, they continue to reward individual efforts and contributions. If teamwork and cooperation are so important, employees should be rewarded for the efforts of the team rather than for their individual roles. Teams win together, and they lose together; they should be rewarded together.

Performance coaches should reward people for the help they give each other. You must not allow individuals to withdraw and isolate themselves from others. You should encourage communications and avoid setting up win–lose competitions between individuals and groups. When cooperation and teamwork are essential, encourage a "we attitude" among employees. It can help you build teamwork through pride and recognition. A team identity is critical in developing teamwork and cooperation.

## BIG NINE: REWARDS THAT ENHANCE COMMITMENT AND GET RESULTS

We believe that there are nine rewards that can help you accomplish each of the strategies previously discussed:

1. Money.
2. Recognition.
3. Sabbaticals.
4. Ownership.
5. Advancement.
6. Freedom and independence.
7. Personal growth opportunities.
8. Fun.
9. Prizes.[3]

### *Money*

Money, money, money, as the song goes, is the greatest of all rewards and is an excellent motivator. Regardless of common knowledge, citing some studies that suggest otherwise, money talks. It is why we all get up in the morning and go to work. Every single day we endure hardships, and money is a big reason we do so. Yes, we understand the importance of challenging and meaningful work and all the other critical career motivators. But we don't discount the importance of the almighty dollar as a reward and as a motivator.

---

[3]Ibid., pp. 97–106.

Money is a meaningful link to improving performance in most jobs. It is a yardstick of success, it represents power and prestige, it is a symbol of our importance, and it is the way many of us keep score. Most organizations that give monetary rewards based on performance do get performance. Let's look at several examples of compensation strategies that organizations can use to get the performance they desire.

**Gainsharing.**   Gainsharing is a pay-for-performance compensation system. It involves groups of employees in improving productivity through better use of human resources, capital, materials, and equipment. In return for their efforts, the organization shares part of the savings from productivity gains with employees. Employees receive cash bonuses (calculated according to some predetermined formula) based on the performance of the group rather than individual performance. Employees are also involved in discovering ways to improve performance and make gains. The strength of gainsharing is that it involves employees in improving performance and has a definite method for determining the portion of the gain each employee will receive.

**Pay-for-knowledge.**   Under a pay-for-knowledge system, base pay and pay increases are tied to job knowledge. Two types of systems are used. "Multi-skills-based" systems tie pay increases to the number of different jobs an employee can perform across the organization. "Increased-knowledge-based" systems tie compensation to the amount of knowledge or range of skills employees possess in a single specialty or job classification.

**Small-group incentives.**   Small-group incentives are a type of gainsharing plan but are based on the performance of a small group of employees rather than an entire department, unit, or division. Another major difference between gainsharing and small group incentives is that incentive programs are usually designed by the organization without employee involvement. Groups of employees do, however, share windfall brought about by improved performance.

**Individual incentives.** When individual incentives are used, all or a portion of an employee's compensation is tied to his or her performance. This system has been used for years in manufacturing and is just now being used in managerial, professional, and service sectors. It is an excellent system for improving individual performance but has very limited effectiveness for encouraging teamwork and cooperation.

**Lump-sum payment bonus.** There are two types of lump-sum plans. First, organizations use lump-sum payments across the board as an alternative to annual automatic percentage increases in base pay. The primary purpose of this approach is to slow the growth in base pay levels. Second, organizations are replacing merit increases with one-time performance bonuses that do not increase an employee's base salary.

**Profit-sharing plans.** Under this plan, employees receive an annual bonus or shares of stock in the organization based on companywide performance. Either employees are paid in cash or their earnings are deferred into a retirement plan.

### Recognition

After money, the second most powerful reward is recognition. Why? Because most of us are egotists and need to be singled out, praised, and appreciated for what we do.

The most important part of recognition is to be genuine. You must mean it when you recognize employees. Your words can't be perceived as coercion or trickery. Recognition must come from the heart. Several examples of recognition are:

- Employee-of-the-month awards for outstanding performance.
- Certificates, trophies, and plaques for achieving important goals.
- Publicity in the form of an article that publicly recognizes the employee.

- Changes in title.
- Honors or awards given at employee banquets.
- Status symbols such as rings and private offices.
- Hall of fame for long-term achievers.
- Charts and posters that tell how well an employee or group is doing a job.
- Praise for a job well done.

## Sabbaticals

For years universities have rewarded their faculties with well-deserved time off to work on special projects and research for outstanding performance. Sabbaticals allow academicians time to recharge their batteries and regain their perspective and bearings. The corporate world should adopt a similar philosophy. A large East Coast management consulting firm allows its employees time to rest and reflect between major client assignments. This is referred to as "being beached." The employees need the time between assignments in order to be fresh for the next challenging experience. According to a senior vice president of human resource development, "This practice helps improve quality and performance."

## Ownership

People with a piece of the action have a stake in the success of an organization. Ownership will positively affect productivity and profitability. However, it requires specific responsibilities such as patience and hard work. It is not a substitute for good management, competitive products and services, a well-conceived marketing plan, an efficient distribution strategy, or competitive advantage. But it does improve cooperation, involvement, and morale.

## Advancement

People who outgrow their organization are forced to leave to acquire greater responsibility and bigger challenges. It is more difficult today to provide opportunities for advancement than it was only 20 years ago. However, lateral transfers to new jobs where employees can broaden their skills and expertise can be an excellent alternative.

Organizations should resist the temptation of promoting people into management unless they have the necessary people and interpersonal skills as well as the managerial insights required to be successful. Otherwise, managerial malpractice will be the ultimate result.

## Freedom and Independence

Highly enterprising employees will welcome the opportunity to obtain freedom and independence as a reward for a job well done. These types of employees will grow and develop when provided with the opportunity to sink their roots deep into the rich soil provided by freedom and independence. Most employees don't mind working harder if they can influence the direction of the ship.

## Personal Growth

For years, training and development have been used as a reward for excellent work. Allowing for personal growth enables employees to use their creative abilities and provides them the opportunity to improve themselves. It is critical to provide training and development activities that are career related so employees can apply what they have learned to the job. Thus, the organization will directly benefit from the advancement of an employee's knowledge and skills. As a result, they both win.

## Fun

Often overlooked as a motivator, fun experiences are truly an incentive. People can endure long hours, unpleasant conditions, and difficult circumstances as long as they enjoy the people they are working with. They want to feel a part of something; it is like having an extended family.

## Prizes

People love to receive gifts and surprises for their contributions. It's exciting to have a prize as an incentive. However, the prizes must be meaningful and fulfilling; they can't be cheap or trivial. It would be better not to give them if they're seen as a joke or embarrassment.

Some good examples of prizes are the following:

- A family dinner paid by the company.
- Theater tickets.
- Tickets to sporting events.
- Vacation trips.
- Gift certificates.
- Company products.
- Bonuses, cash, or merchandise.

Improving performance is a complex and difficult process. You have a tremendous responsibility to provide the most appropriate reward strategy for your employees. Remember, the things that get rewarded, get done. This simple philosophy will work wonders in improving employee performance and getting the results you want.

# Index